Anglican Church-Building in London

1946–2012

Michael Yelton

with photographs by

John Salmon

Spire Books Ltd

PO Box 2336, Reading RG4 5WJ
www.spirebooks.com

Publication of this book was assisted by a donation from the
Anglo-Catholic History Society

Spire Books Ltd
PO Box 2336, Reading RG4 5WJ
www.spirebooks.com

Printed by By Berforts Information Press

ISBN 978-1-904965-44-2

CONTENTS

INTRODUCTION
Michael Yelton

This book is a sequel to an earlier volume on Anglican church-building in London between 1915 and 1945, which was published in 2007 and is in a similar format. The long delay between the two volumes is attributable to a surprising statistic of which even the authors were unaware until work began on this book: namely that during the period in question as many as 250 new churches were built in Greater London, or in a few cases older buildings were substantially reconstructed. That very large corpus of work has been largely overlooked by commentators and in particular the replacements for the very substantial number of Victorian suburban churches which have been demolished in recent years have been as little mentioned as have the older buildings which have been lost.

The aim of this volume is similar to its predecessor: to provide a gazetteer of and introduction to new Anglican church-building in what is now the Greater London area, in this case from 1946 to 2012.

The Greater London area is convenient, not only because it is clearly defined and widely understood, but also it corresponds generally to the built-up metropolitan area. The decision to confine the book to Anglican churches, as with the previous volume, was taken to restrict a very large subject to a publishable core. In some ways a comparison between the way in which the various churches (particularly the Roman Catholic, which experienced a very large surge in the provision of new buildings over this period) dealt with changes in the light of new liturgical insights would have been helpful and is a potential subject for further research in due course.

Interest is undoubtedly growing in the work of some modern architects, particularly the ground-breaking partnership of Maguire & Murray, on whom a full-length study by Gerald Adler was published in 2012. However, although their work and St Paul, Bow Common in particular, is featured in many commentaries, little regard is paid to how few followed in the path they had set out. Just as St Saviour, Eltham, by N.F. Cachemaille-Day, is regarded as the archetypal interwar church, but in fact was not much copied, St Paul, Bow Common stands on its own in many respects. Maguire & Murray only built one other church in London, St Joseph the Worker, Northolt, which was very different in many respects and they designed very few elsewhere.

There appears to be no interest hitherto in the work of most of the other architects who flourished in the post–Second World War period, even in the post–St Paul, Bow Common era. Biscoe & Stanton, for example, a practice founded by Michael Biscoe in 1966, designed a considerable number of modern churches around London in the 1971-80 period, which have been little discussed.

That neglect is even more marked in the case of buildings constructed in the 1950s, which have been subjected to considerable vilification, particularly from Nikolaus Pevsner and his successors, on the grounds that they were too backward-looking in their design and in their execution. However, they reflected the mood of the times and of the man and woman in the pew, and they have now matured with use.

Architects such as Thomas Francis Ford (1891-1971) and Ralph G.C. Covell (1911-88), both of whom were responsible for many new churches, particularly in the Diocese of Southwark, have received little praise and much opprobrium. Perhaps the least attractive church in the eyes of many critics is Covell's St Agnes, Kennington Park, which was erected in 1956. Sir John Betjeman was mortified by the refusal of the Southwark diocesan authorities to rebuild George Gilbert Scott junior's masterly church, which had been damaged by bombing, but not so badly that it could not have been rebuilt. Many others of its era which were just as badly affected were later reconstructed. He made his views very clear in the dedication of his *Collins Pocket Guide to English Churches*. More recently Anthony Symondson, in his monograph on Stephen Dykes-Bower, has commented loftily that the behaviour of the Diocese in not rebuilding was 'scandalous' and that 'the noblest and most beautiful church of the late Gothic Revival' was replaced by a 'humble substitute'.[1]

However, comments to that effect pay insufficient regard to the reality of ecclesiastical life in areas which have been substantially depopulated since 1945 and where many of those who remain living there are not well off. If St Agnes had indeed been reconstructed so as to rival its former glory, from where would the congregation have come? From whose pockets would the church have been maintained? It could only have been rebuilt had the decision been taken to make it the only church in the vicinity, instead of allowing the construction of, for example, the fine new St Paul, Lorrimore Square, Walworth, and the rather less impressive St Mary, Newington, both of which are only a stone's throw away.

While no-one would suggest that Covell's replacement is a masterpiece, it is compact, easy to maintain, and of an appropriate size for the locale and it is clear from the way in which it is kept internally that it is appreciated. In Battersea during the same period, Ford designed Christ Church, which although not an immediately memorable sight externally, has acquired in a relatively short time a feeling of welcome and of holiness which other more distinguished buildings lack.

A particular problem affects the ambit of this book, which is the substantial reconstruction of churches in circumstances where parts of the former building were used. This has occurred frequently, both to deal with wartime damage and as part of more modern reductions in capacity and the provision of ancillary accommodation. In general terms, those where a comprehensive reconstruction has taken place, as opposed to a mere reordering, are included, whereas those which were patched up, sometimes quite extensively, after the War, are not. In the City, where a very high proportion of the churches were damaged by bombing, two which were very extensively rebuilt receive special mention, but the subject as a whole is really outside the focus of this book. Inevitably there are some churches elsewhere which have been included which some may think should have been left out and vice versa and there are some special cases, such as St Matthew, Bethnal Green. This was rebuilt in accordance with the original plans, but internally it was redecorated and refurnished to a very high standard, but in accordance with the standards of the time and using many of the promising church furnishers then available. Thus it clearly should be included within this study. St Stephen, Canonbury, is another such example.

Church-building in the period in question falls into three broad categories:

1. The replacement of churches which had been damaged in the Second World War, and in a few cases by fire or the like subsequently.

2. The provision of new buildings for areas which were being developed for housing.

3. The replacement of large older, usually Victorian, edifices by smaller, new constructions, often on part of the old site and nearly always with the provision of ancillary accommodation within the same framework.

It is clear that the number of churches in the second category is perhaps less than might be expected, whereas those in the first and third categories, especially the third, are found more frequently than generally envisaged. In the interwar period there had been a huge expansion of the London built-up area, largely in Middlesex and in Essex, with a corresponding growth in churches required for those moving into the newly developed estates, in a large ring around London. After 1945, this did not happen in anything like the same way. The combination of the imposition of the Green Belt and of the establishment of the New Towns in a circle around, but outside of, London, relieved the pressure on land within what is now the Greater London area. The real problem in many localities was not increasing but decreasing population and that decline has only been addressd relatively recently by, for example, the redevelopment of the Docklands. Stepney for example had a population of 298,600 in 1901 and began closing churches as early as 1911; by 1951 only 99,000 lived in the then borough.

The depopulation of many urban areas was not properly considered by the church authorities and particularly not by the Diocese of Southwark. The Diocese of London appears to have been more realistic about the need for replacement churches in the East End. An order under the Reorganization Area Measure was made in relation to the Stepney parishes in 1951, well before any rebuilding started. Relatively few new buildings were erected in Tower Hamlets and many parishes were amalgamated. In fact even the decision to replace St Paul, Bow Common by the much-praised new design was not universally welcomed. Gordon Barnes, the historian of the local churches and a well-known ecclesiologist, says rather pointedly that the new building is 'completely different from its predecessor, and has indeed provoked much comment and criticism'.[2] The Revd Basil F.L. Clarke, whose knowledge of churches in London was profound, recorded his thoughts about St Paul's privately in his notebook, as detailed in the gazetteer which follows, hiding them somewhat in his entry in his *Parish Churches of London*.

Although there was much less greenfield building after 1945, there was some and the Church tried to establish a presence at an early stage in, for example, Harold Hill (Havering), New Addington (Croydon), Thames View (Barking) and later Thamesmead (Greenwich).

The real underlying problem was, of course, lack of money and, in the immediate post-war era, a shortage of building materials. The age of rich private donors, which largely disappeared in 1914, had by this time gone completely.

After the War, there was also a significant temporal gap before any new buildings, other than the purely temporary, came into being. The economic state of the country and the need to obtain scarce building permits were high hurdles for the promoters of any new scheme to vault. The first new church in the London area appears to have been Holy Cross, Motspur Park, in 1949. There were a number of others, which were mainly in new areas of development where the need was urgent, but replacement of those which had been destroyed in the War was painfully slow.

One of the really significant failures of the diocesan authorities was not to be able to provide replacement churches for those destroyed or damaged until the late 1950s, some fifteen years after the destruction of the original buildings. In the meantime congregations had dispersed, or been accommodated elsewhere, so by the time the new church was ready for use, the parishioners were not there. It does appear retrospectively that there was a determination to rebuild and that once the decision to do so had been taken, there was a reluctance to reconsider in the light of the changing circumstances whether it remained viable to provide yet more accommodation.

That depressing tendency was accentuated as the years went by with the influx of non-Christians to the inner urban areas, and also by the inability or unwillingness of the Church of England to attract and retain those immigrating from the West Indies and elsewhere who had been brought up to attend church regularly.

The clearest example of over-provision can be found in those areas of south London near the river. More than 20 new churches have been built since 1945 in the modern Borough of Southwark. Some of those have seen very little use. St Crispin, Bermondsey was completed in 1959 and made redundant in 1999: it is now used as a nursery. All Saints & St Stephen, Walworth, replaced the two churches of those names. It was designed by the distinguished and prolific ecclesiastical architect Cachemaille-Day and was also opened in 1959. It was made redundant as early as 1975 and within two years was being seriously considered for demolition. Instead, it was in due course sold to a Nigerian sect and remains standing.

St Andrew, Waterloo, was a traditional building designed by the well-known firm of D.E. Nye & Partners and opened in 1960. By 2003 it was declared redundant and was then demolished and replaced on a different site by a multi-purpose building with a small 'worship area'. All Hallows, Southwark, was a large and stately church by George Gilbert Scott junior which was badly damaged by bombing. Instead of rebuilding or demolishing it, the Diocese steered an unsatisfactory middle path, namely the reconstruction of one chapel only. That too was relatively soon declared redundant and the site is now the subject of much local debate.

The Diocese of London, although apparently more organised than its counterpart to the south, was not immune from similar problems. St Nicholas & All Hallows, Poplar was opened in 1955 and closed again as early as 1968, although after some 30 years as a store, it was refurbished and reopened in 1997.

The failure to appreciate the needs of the neighbourhoods involved became even more acute after about 1960. Although the over-provision of new churches was largely in relation to replacements for those which had been war-damaged, the steep decline in church-going after that time, which contrasted with a small but steady growth in the 1950s and an increase over that period in vocations, leading to a false optimism, led to the early demise of some buildings. St Mary, Charlton, was not constructed until 1961, was vacated as early as 1974 and then demolished. An even more poignant example is St George with St Andrew, Battersea. After both the original churches were bombed and demolished, followed by a long period in which the congregation worshipped in a temporary building, a large new church by Covell was erected in 1955-6, with a tower proclaiming its presence to the area. By 1996 the body of the church had been demolished and replaced by a much smaller building, although the tower was kept.

In Cricklewood a new church known as Little St Peter was opened in 1958 to designs by Braddock & Martin-Smith. It was carefully thought out and had some interesting fittings. As early as 1983 it was closed and has not been used for worship since.

There is also no doubt that there was a significant change in buildings which were constructed after about 1960, with many more new ideas coming to the fore.

The best contemporary source-book for the period before 1960 is the volume published by the Incorporated Church Building Society in 1956 and entitled *Sixty Post-war Churches*, depicting buildings all over England which had been erected since about 1951. It laid particular emphasis on what was becoming an increasing trend towards hall/churches with a dual purpose use. Prior to the Second World War, many halls had been erected for worship in developing areas, as precursors to a church. In some cases such a church was indeed constructed after 1945, for example St Mary, Isleworth, and St Swithun, Purley (where work had begun on the church before 1939 and was then restarted to a different design in the early 1950s).

After 1945, the emphasis changed so that a hall/church suitable for secular as well as religious activities was positively promoted as a solution for new areas of housing, although interestingly Martin-Smith (who had before the War designed the then forward-thinking John Keble Church, Mill Hill) in his introduction to the ICBS book, rather decried the idea. What was certainly the case was that many hall/churches were built in the 1951-60 period, a large number of which are still in use.

It would be idle to assert that, even if churches built in the 1950s are in need of reappraisal and renewed interest, they are architectural masterpieces. What is undoubtedly the case is that they were generally constructed along traditional lines, even if using modern building materials and methods, without reference to new theological and liturgical thinking. Very few new churches reflected the influence of the Liturgical Movement and its desire to see the priest and people worshipping as part of the same community around the altar. Perhaps the most significant exception to that is the interesting church of All Saints, Hanworth, which was designed by none other than Cachemaille-Day. There is no doubt also that church-building in England over that period was inward looking and little regard was given to the developments in France, Germany, Switzerland and other countries in Europe, where new buildings were being constructed, generally by the Roman Catholic church, which were internally bare and focused on an altar situated well forward of the east wall, so that the priest was part of the congregation instead of separated from them.

A number of churches over this period were in fact designed by those who had started work, or in some cases done their best work, before 1939. Ford had designed several halls and churches in the 1930s and between 1953 and 1960 he supervised the construction of a further eleven in London, nearly all in the Diocese of Southwark. J. Harold Gibbons, who had been responsible for a number of significant and well-considered churches between the wars, produced another three in the 1950s. Sir Edward Maufe designed two (St Alphege, Edmonton, and St Augustine of Canterbury, Whitton) in a style which had changed little since St Thomas, Hanwell, in the 1930s. Seely & Paget were another firm which was already well-known before the War, but continued in practice thereafter in a generally conservative way, including the interesting and careful rebuilding of St Andrew, Holborn.

Sir Ninian Comper built no new churches in London or elsewhere after the War, but his son Sebastian built two replacements for bombed buildings (St Helen, North Kensington, and St Matthew, Wimbledon), reconstructed St John, East Dulwich, and greatly extended St John the Evangelist, Coulsdon. However, the spirit of the times was against the devotion to beauty which marked the Compers' outlook, especially that of the father, and also against the expenditure required to put their ideas into effect.

Nugent Cachemaille-Day, a man always ingenious and never able to be placed in a particular category, is usually considered as primarily an interwar architect, largely on the strength of St Saviour, Eltham, and his work of the same period in Manchester. However, he designed no fewer than nine churches in London between 1952 and 1964, one of which (St Peter, Lee) has already been demolished. These include at least two of considerable distinction, namely St James, Clapham Park, and St Michael & All Angels, London Fields. Others still active in the 1950s included Caroe & Partners and D.E. Nye & Partners. Romilly Craze, perhaps like Ford and Covell, an underrated figure, designed seven churches in London, some much criticised for being uninspired. The Chelmsford Diocesan architect, J.J. Crowe, continued producing churches on the Essex side of London, at least two of which (St Nicholas, Elm Park, and St Francis of Assisi, Barkingside) were extraordinarily retrospective in appearance.

The number of prominent new ecclesiastical architects in the 1950s was very small, which is perhaps surprising given the amount of work which was then available. One of the more interesting is Michael Farey, whose father Cyril designed a number of churches between the Wars. Michael Farey started off in a fairly conservative mode, with St Andrew, Roxbourne, and the Good Shepherd, West Hounslow, but by the end of the 1950s he had produced the much more modern St Luke, West Kilburn, and later he designed Christ the Redeemer, Southall, which drew on the ideas behind Bow Common.

Even the Gothic Revival had not expired, as can be seen for example by the substantial extension and rebuilding of All Saints, Orpington, by Geddes Hyslop in 1957-8. Before the War he had designed a far more revolutionary design in the Bishop Andrewes Church, St Helier. Romilly Craze's replacement of the bombed church of St. Mark, Surbiton, was as late as 1960 but could almost have dated from 1910.

All this began to change about 1960. The construction of St Paul, Bow Common, in 1958-60, although of great significance, was a consequence of changing attitudes rather than a catalyst for them. In 1957 the New Churches Research Group was founded, largely on the initiative of the Revd Peter Hammond (1921-99), then rector of Bagendon, Gloucestershire, later a teacher of art in Hull, and still later a canon of Lincoln Cathedral. In 1960 Hammond published *Liturgy and Architecture*, which was widely publicised and read and was an extremely influential book in the field. In 1962 he followed this with a collection of essays contributed by members of the NCRG, including Robert Maguire, Keith Murray, and Nigel Melhuish, later to be the architect of St Stephen, Wandsworth (1981), St Philip the Apostle, Sydenham (1984), and Immanuel & St Andrew, Streatham (1989). This was entitled *Towards a Church Architecture*.

It was, however, the first of the two books which made the greatest impact and certainly pulled no punches. Hammond had convinced himself that the problem with church architecture was lack of consideration for the purpose of the building and continued adherence to the clericalist theories promoted with such success by the Ecclesiologists. He saw the Liturgical Movement as the only way to proceed and, in his own essay in *Towards a Church Architecture*, he was very critical of Peter F. Anson, whose well-known book *Fashions in Church Furnishings 1840-1940* had recently been published, for suggesting that it was merely a passing phase, following on a variety of others which he had chronicled.

In *Liturgy and Architecture* Hammond was very critical indeed of the buildings constructed in England since 1945. After commenting that many churches had been built in the 1950-60 period he commented: 'The results of all this activity have been depressing in the extreme'.[3] He went on to describe his reactions to what was set out in *Sixty Post-war Churches* thus: 'There is little to choose between the unimaginative drabness of the dual purpose churches, with their tawdry furnishings, and the empty pretentiousness of the more ambitious buildings'.[4] Later he poured scorned on those who had adopted modern materials but not modern theological insights: 'some of the very worst churches of the last thirty years are those which strive resolutely after a contemporary idiom. Nothing is easier – or more irrelevant – than to disguise what is basically a nineteenth century church in contemporary fancy-dress'.[5]

Hammond was making a case, but it may be that he grossly overstated the position. Certainly, we can perhaps now look back on some churches of the 1950s with something approaching appreciation. He, however, would have none of it. Churches should not only be built of modern materials, they should express the principles of liturgical renewal. He was commendatory of some such as Comper who might be regarded by others as reactionary, and also of Cachemaille-Day, whom nobody could regard as other than a thinker and innovator. He was not certain of the virtues of a central altar and his main concern was the reproduction, even in modern forms, of earlier designs based on medieval or Ecclesiological principles.

St Paul, Bow Common, reflected completely the new insights brought to bear by the Liturgical Movement, with some idiosyncratic insight from the parish priest, the Revd R. Gresham Kirkby. The altar was placed forward, with movable seats around it and the walls were bare. It was top lit. The entire building was constructed of cheap industrial materials, in complete contradistinction to the Victorian belief that churches should be constructed with the very best available.

Many of the churches constructed in the post-1960 period have in fact been replacements for large and, by then, crumbling Victorian buildings which had become too difficult to maintain. This tendency appears to have been little noticed, although the number of buildings concerned is very large, particularly in the Diocese of Southwark. It is also important to understand that there have been very few architects who have designed many such churches. There have conversely been many who have designed just one or two. The exceptions to the generality of that statement are Biscoe & Stanton, as already mentioned, who constructed eight churches in Greater London between 1971 and 1980, many of which were in unusual special forms and nearly all of which incorporated further buildings or housing on the site of the old church, and APEC, who between 1983 and 1994 constructed or reconstructed eight churches in East London, nearly all in the Borough of Newham. The initiative by the Diocese of Chelmsford was brought about by the need to reduce drastically the number of seats available for the congregations in an area in which so many non-Christians were then living.

This tendency was also manifest in other areas. However, there were some new buildings which were undoubtedly striking. St Paul, Harringay, built under the supervision of Peter Jenkins in 1988-93, has been highly praised for its ingenuity and force of design and has many fine contemporary fittings. After a disastrous fire, All Saints, West Dulwich, was restored by Thomas F. Ford & Partners in what may be described as a modern Gothic image.

There is of course another side to every argument. One of the churches praised by Peter Hammond was St Mary Magdalene, Peckham, which was in the course of being planned when his books were published. The new building, by Potter & Hare, was erected in 1962 and had a prominent position in an island on a cross-roads. However, although Hammond was delighted with the thought which had gone into the design, the roof leaked and this and other defects which became apparent in actual use of the building, led to its demolition and replacement after less than 50 years.

It may also be that in England the Liturgical Movement, although regarded by some traditionalist Anglo-Catholics as almost heretical, a stance which became more difficult to maintain once the Second Vatican Council had pronounced, was more influenced by streams within the successors of the Oxford Movement than has sometimes been appreciated. Father Gresham Kirkby himself was the curious combination of political devotion to anarchy or communism, but theological adherence to some very conservative tenets. In his earlier years he was a supporter of the Annunciation Group, which campaigned against the inter-denominational Church of South India. In his later years he was a member of Forward in Faith and thus a strong opponent of women clergy. One of the other propagandists for the New Churches Research Group was the Revd Patrick McLaughlin, who later went over to Rome.

Although the Anglo-Catholic Movement went into relative decline, particularly after 1960, its traditions were sustained with surprising strength in the churches built in the period in question. It may be that this was because many of the churches were replacements for others and many were in inner city areas. It was, perhaps understandably, regarded as important to retain the loyalty of existing members by recreating, although in different surroundings, the worship to which they had been accustomed. Thus the new small St Agnes, Kennington Park, continued the traditions established in its far more spacious and awe-inspiring predecessor. In more recent years, it has nearly always been the case that when a large but decayed Victorian church has been demolished and a modern replacement of one third of the size has been erected, the tone of the worship has continued. Thus in the churches in this volume, Anglo-Catholic ideas have proved more tenacious than might be expected. The well-known concept that the Oxford Movement found it difficult to establish itself in the suburbs is shown by the contrast between these churches, which are often not suburban, and those in the earlier volume, which largely were and which were nearly all central in their churchmanship.

There were also a few architects practising in the period who identified themselves to a greater or lesser degree with Anglo-Catholicism. Cachemaille-Day was one, although he was never backward-looking in his ideas. Romilly Craze, who was closely associated through his partner Sir William Milner with the Walsingham Shrine, was another. Laurence King, who designed a number of suburban churches, was also closely involved at Walsingham.

If Anglo-Catholicism was to prove more adaptable than might at first sight appear, Evangelicalism has flourished among the newer churches. A fundamentalist presentation of the Faith appears to have more success in attracting a committed core, particularly in new areas, than has middle-of-the-road Anglicanism. This has meant that the interiors in particular of many of the churches constructed in the era have very little interest. In fact in some, virtually all the expected fittings are either non-existent or have been pushed aside, often in favour of musical instruments. There is a stark bareness in many of these churches which is totally different from the planned lack of furnishings which was a hallmark of the more extreme proponents of the Liturgical Movement. Some, such as St Luke, Cranham Park, have been so successful in attracting congregations that a new larger church has been required, in that case in 2002, resulting in the demolition of the 1957 building. Others have continued with declining numbers but usually optimism.

Some churches, particularly those of an Evangelical persuasion, have been reordered so that the focus is on the north or south (in other words one of the longer walls) which enables the congregation to see and hear the preacher, but totally destroys the original design.

The last few years have not shown any great consistency in the design of new churches. Although the Liturgical Movement has had a widespread effect on all churches, the concept that its ideas would overtake all others has proved not to be the case. However, there have been individual churches which are vibrant and striking, such as St Antony with St Silas, Nunhead; St Barnabas, Dulwich; St George, Perry Hill; and St Paul, Harringay.

The main part of this book is a gazetteer by area, for which purpose the churches have been set out, as already stated, by reference to the London borough in which they stand, which it is hoped is the most readily comprehensible form of organisation. They are also cross-referenced to the relevant volumes of the *Buildings of England, London* (noted as Pevsner 1 and so on), to *Sixty Post-war Churches,* to Basil Clarke's well-known work and to other books.

However, it was also thought that it would be helpful, as in our earlier volume, to list the architects and firms with a cross-reference to the churches they designed. For some buildings, especially those designed as halls, the name of the architect has not been established and they are therefore in the main gazetteer, but not in the list of architects.

The authors are most grateful to the many priests, vergers and key-holders who have allowed them access and it is no reflection on them that some of the interiors, particularly where buildings are now used for secular purposes, are not thought worthy of reproduction.

Notes

1. A. Symondson, *Stephen Dykes Bower*, London, pp. 118-19.
2. G. Barnes, *Stepney Churches: an Historical Account*, London, 1967, p. 97.
3. P. Hammond, *Liturgy and Architecture*, London, 1960, p. 1.
4. Ibid., p. 2.
5. Ibid., p. 6.

REFERENCES

Clarke   B.F.L. Clarke, *Parish Churches of London*, London, 1966.

Leonard   John Leonard, *London's Parish Churches*, Reading, 2011.

Pevsner, 1   Simon Bradley & Nikolaus Pevsner, *The Buildings of England: London 1: The City of London*, London, 1997.

Pevsner, 2   Bridget Cherry & Nikolaus Pevsner, *The Buildings of England: London 2: South*, Harmondsworth, 1983.

Pevsner, 3   Bridget Cherry & Nikolaus Pevsner, *The Buildings of England: London 3: North West*, London, 1991.

Pevsner, 4   Bridget Cherry & Nikolaus Pevsner, *The Buildings of England: London 4: North*, London, London, 1998.

Pevsner, 5   Bridget Cherry, Charles O'Brien & Nikolaus Pevsner, *The Buildings of England: London 5: East*, London, 2005.

Pevsner, 6   Simon Bradley & Nikolaus Pevsner, *The Buildings of England: London 6: Westminster*, London, 2003.

SPWC   Incorporated Church Building Society, *Sixty Post-war Churches*, London, 1956.

Barking & Dagenham

Christ Church, Barking

Status: in use.

Location: Bastable Avenue, south side, near western junction with Curzon Crescent.

Nearest station: Upney.

Constructed: 1958.

Architect: not known.

Christ Church was constructed as one of the centrepieces of the almost self-contained Thames View Estate, in a prominent position: its visual impact is further increased by the presence of a substantial bell-tower. The tower marks it for what it is: otherwise the building is a plain brick hall, without aisles, well lit by clear windows. The sanctuary is underfurnished in accordance with the Evangelical ethos of the locality, and can be shut off from the remainder of the building to allow secular use of the nave.

Reference: Pevsner, 5, p. 136.

St Cedd, Becontree

Status: in use.

Location: Lodge Avenue, east side, north of junction with Bromhall Road.

Nearest station: Becontree.

Constructed: 1963.

Architects: Thompson & Whitehead.

This church replaced a temporary church of 1936. The foundation stone was laid by the local MP, Tom Driberg, who was a strong Anglo-Catholic: however, the church is Evangelical. The church is small and brick-built, in a cruciform shape with a copper roof and a small flèche. The interior has lurid colours, which match the abstract stained glass windows.

Reference: Pevsner, 5, p. 141.

St Erkenwald, Barking

Status: in use.

Location: Levett Road, south side, near Upney Lane junction.

Nearest station: Upney.

Constructed: 1954.

Architect: R.C. Foster of Tooley & Foster.

This church was constructed to replace a temporary building, which now serves as a hall. It is a more distinguished church than many of its time, with a saddle-back tower and a large porch with a semi-circular cast-iron relief over the door depicting St Erkenwald. The architect also designed many of the interior fittings. The chief glory of the building is, however, two sets of glass by John Hutton, dated 1955 and 1968 respectively and of contrasting style, with the earlier group (in lancets) more gentle in form than the later (in the nave aisles). They contrast with the relatively bare interior. This is an interesting and little-known building which was recently refurbished.

Reference: Pevsner, 5, p. 124.

St John the Divine, Dagenham

Status: in use.

Location: Goresbrook Road, north side, near junction with Canonsleigh Road.

Nearest station: Becontree.

Constructed: 1986.

Architect: not known.

This is the third church to bear this name. In 1936 A.E. Wiseman built a distinguished basilica, which was demolished after a life of only 50 years and replaced by this building, which is small and thus more manageable, built of brick, with a square clerestory and sloping roofs, above domestic style full-length windows.

St Mark, Chadwell Heath

Status: in use.

Location: Rose Lane, corner Arneways Avenue.

Nearest station: Chadwell Heath.

Constructed: 1956.

Architect: not known.

This is a small brick-built church in a somewhat depressing area north of Eastern Avenue. The church, which is very low, is overshadowed by the surrounding three-storey flats around. The roof is green, as is the tiny bell-tower surmounted by a cross, and there is a substantial porch with columns. The interior can be described as functional Evangelical, without any distinction: it is also used as a hall.

Reference: Pevsner, 5, p. 147

Other Churches

Hartley Brook Church, Dagenham

A small brick-built Evangelical hall was constructed in 1955 in Rosslyn Avenue, between Chadwell Heath and Becontree Heath, which remains in use. It is an offshoot of St Mary, Becontree.

Heath Park Church, Dagenham

Part of the Community Hall in Rusholme Avenue, Becontree Heath, has been used as a church, but no longer is. It is a simple brick-built building.

St Paul, Barking

The church, in Ripple Road, was hit by a flying bomb and demolished. A replacement was built in 1956 to designs by D.F. Martin-Smith, which is referred to in different sources both as St Paul and as a hall of St Margaret, the parish church. It was used for only a short time.

Barnet

Little St Peter, Cricklewood

Status: now incorporated into an old people's home.
Location: Claremont Way, north side.
Nearest station: Brent Cross.
Constructed: 1958.
Architect: Braddock & Martin-Smith.
This church had a remarkably short life. It was opened in 1958 and was carefully designed. It is a small polygonal building topped by a very high pinnacle with a cross. It featured two stained glass windows and an external brick sculpture of St Peter, all by Jack Baker. However by 1983 so little use was being made of the building that it was closed and has now been taken into an adjoining care home, although still displaying signs of its past, including the cross aloft.

Reference: SPWC, pp. 88-9.

St Augustine, Grahame Park

Status: in use.
Location: Great Field.
Nearest station: Colindale.
Constructed: 1975.
Architect: Biscoe & Stanton.

This church was built to serve a new estate developed on the former airfield. It has considerable similarities to many Roman Catholic churches erected at the same time, not least because the worship and fittings are strongly Anglo-Catholic. Biscoe & Stanton produced a design very typical of its era: polygonal, of red/blue brick, with high windows and then a tent roof with small belfry above. The altar is pulled forward from a traditional position, with chairs in a semi-circle. There is a statue of the patron saint holding a model of the church, and fittings which tone in with the building.

Reference: Pevsner, 4, p. 157.

St Matthias, Colindale

Status: in use.
Location: St Matthias Close, off Rushgrove Avenue.
Nearest station: Hendon.
Constructed: 1973.
Architect: R.W. Hurst.

This replaced an adjoining building, now used as a hall. It has a rather spiky outline in brick and slate with very high windows in the west side of the roof: the east wall has slits to cast light on the altar and there is a separate baptistery. The fittings are Anglo-Catholic.

Reference: Pevsner, 4, p. 159.

Other Churches

St Peter, Cricklewood

The former church in Cricklewood Lane, built in 1891, was demolished in the 1970s: services were transferred to the former parish hall, which was adapted in 1977 for use as the church, not least by inserting crude dormer windows in the roof. In 2003 this was sold and the parish now has no church of its own but uses a brick hall in Claremont Road ('New St Peter's').

St Peter, Edgware

In 1963 a small brick hall was constructed in Stone Grove, with a detached wooden frame from which is hung a bell and a cross. The furnishings are Evangelical.

Reference: Pevsner, 4, p. 157.

Bexley

Bishop Ridley Church, Welling

Status: in use.

Location: The Green, north side, between two arms of Falconwood Parade.

Nearest station: Falconwood.

Constructed: 1957-8.

Architect: not known.

As its dedication would imply, this has always been an ultra-Evangelical church. It has little architectural distinction, being built of red brick with slightly pitched roofs and substantial but plain glass windows. The roof does have a small cupola. The interior is basically rectangular but has been reordered so that the seats are in a semi-circle around the lectern, with the holy table against the wall behind. All walls are white. An entrance porch which resembles a conservatory has been added.

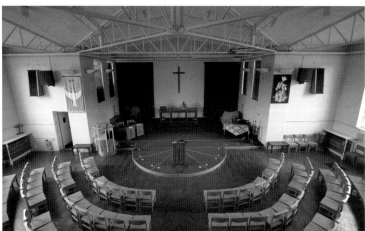

St Andrew, Bostall Heath

Status: in use.
Location: Brampton Road, corner of Abbotts Walk.
Nearest station: Abbey Wood.
Constructed: 1956-7.
Architect: not known.

This church replaced a wooden building erected in 1935, which was constructed as a result of a substantial increase in housing around. Money for the new church was raised locally. It has a striking external appearance, with tall very steeply pitched roofs with visible beams inside. The sanctuary is plain but there is a very large cross above the altar on the elevated east wall. There are large clear windows on the west wall and on both nave walls.

St Andrew, Sidcup
Status: in use.
Location: Maylands Drive, corner of St Andrew's Road.
Nearest station: Albany Park.
Constructed: 1964.
Architect: Braddock, Martin-Smith & Lipley.
This small church shows how new ideas of design were moving into vogue by
the 1960s. The editors of Pevsner say it is 'ingenious, fashionable, and slightly
absurd', which is not unfair. The building is octagonal and set on a slope so that
the church (above) is reached via a bridge from the road: beneath is the parish
room. It replaced a hall opened in 1946. The roof has eight sections, alternately
very steeply pitched or tall gables. There is a thin spire above. Inside, the altar
remains near the east wall, as opposed to being placed centrally, and there are few
furnishings, in accordance with Evangelical practice.

Reference: Pevsner, 2, pp. 148-9.

St Mary, Welling

Status: in use.
Location: Wickham Street, west side, north of Sandringham Drive corner.
Nearest station: Welling.
Constructed: 1954.
Architect: Thomas F. Ford.
The editors of Pevsner sniff at this building, saying: 'a building like this epitomizes all that mid-C20 architecture ought not to be'. However, as usual with Ford's designs, it is well thought out and has lasted. It is in very red brick, with some nods to early Christian buildings, and a Lombardic tower. Inside, the building has some eighteenth-century detail, with a neat sanctuary, and narrow aisles with round-headed arches on each side, all in white but relieved by pastel blue. There is a mural by Hans Feibusch behind the altar, and further wall paintings by Clare Dawson. It replaced a hall/church next door.

Reference: Pevsner, 2, p. 152.

St Peter, Bexleyheath

Status: in use.

Location: Pickford Lane, corner Bristow Road.

Nearest station: Bexleyheath.

Constructed: 1957.

Architect: Thomas F. Ford.

This is rather different from most designs by Ford: it is cruciform in layout, with a slightly elevated roof covering the central area and separate roofs for each of the four arms. The interior has a conventionally placed sanctuary, with behind it three murals by Feibusch, who also decorated the ceiling. There is a separate chapel.

Other Churches

Good Shepherd, Blackfen

A small church was erected in 1967 to serve part of the parish of the Holy Redeemer, Lamorbey, with a hall area and a chancel: the plain building has an elevated roof. Regular services ceased in 1990 and it is now used only for community purposes.

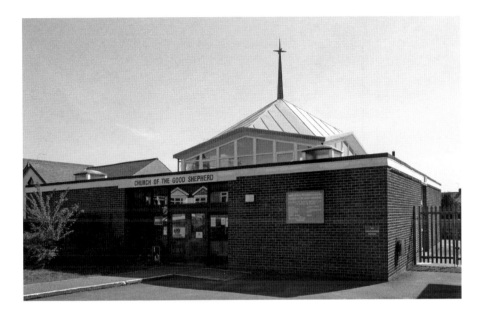

Brent

All Saints, Queensbury

Status: in use.

Location: Waltham Drive, corner Brinkburn Gardens.

Nearest station: Queensbury.

Constructed: 1954.

Architect: R. B. Craze.

The editors of Pevsner give one of their shortest descriptions of this church: 'brick'. That is certainly true. It was constructed to replace temporary buildings and as with many early post-war churches was built in a similar style to those before 1939. This is a substantial building of almost unrelieved red brick, hence Pevsner's comment, but it has real presence and a feeling of permanence. Using neo-Romanesque round arches and with a short north west tower it has slit windows in the nave and a circular window over the western entrance.

References: Pevsner, 3, p. 135; SPWC, p. 49.

Annunciation, South Kenton

Status: in use.
Location: Windermere Avenue, west side, near junction with Carlton Avenue East
Nearest station: South Kenton.
Constructed: 1961.
Architects: Riley & Glanfield.
This church looks externally similar to a hall, with a multitude of windows on two levels. Internally, it has both wall painting and stained glass by the distinguished artist John Hayward. There is a tin hall in front which was the former church.

Reference: Pevsner, 3, pp. 132–3.

Ascension, Preston

Status: in use.

Location: The Avenue, west side, opposite West Close.

Nearest station: Preston Road.

Constructed: 1957.

Architect: J. Harold Gibbons.

This was probably the last church designed by Gibbons, who died in 1958. It was paid for largely by the moneys paid as a result of the destruction of St Saviour, Ealing, and it replaced a hall erected in 1937. It is typical of Gibbons in that it is carefully thought out and detailed: it is built in yellow brick with a small stone cupola above on the east side, and is much more reminiscent of his pre-war designs than some of his other churches. There is inside a wall painting by Hans Feibusch, executed some years before and some stained glass by W. Carter Shapland and others.

Reference: Pevsner, 3, p. 141.

St Augustine, Wembley Park

Status: in use.

Location: Forty Lane, corner Bridge Road.

Nearest station: Wembley Park.

Constructed: 1953.

Architects: W. Wylton Todd and Guy Biscoe.

The spectacularly unsuccessful church by T.H. Lyon, erected as recently as 1926, was demolished as early as 1950 after it was found to be unsafe and was replaced by this much simpler building, which was originally intended to be a hall and to be replaced by another permanent church, which has never been built. It is a rectangular brick building with a barrel roof and a small chancel at the east end: in 1979 a lobby was added at the north-western corner of the nave, leading to a vestry with a small tower and belfry. The reredos behind the high altar incorporates figures by Lyon from the earlier church and that behind the south west chapel is also from the same source: both are disproportionately large for this building. There are also statues from the earlier building: an Anglo-Catholic tradition has been maintained. Stained glass was introduced in the 1960s.

St Cuthbert, North Wembley

Status: in use.

Location: Carlton Avenue West, corner Watford Road.

Nearest station: South Kenton.

Constructed: 1958.

Architect: R.B. Craze.

This is a design by an underrated architect. Craze produced a yellow brick building, tall but without tower, with a shallow pitched roof and a substantial 14 light west window. The trusses beneath the roof are pierced with circles in an unusual touch. There is a powerful mural behind the altar by Harper & Hendra.

Reference: Pevsner, 3, p. 141.

St James, Alperton

Status: in use.
Location: Stanley Avenue, south side, west of Lightley Close.
Nearest station: Alperton.
Constructed: 1990.
Architect: Anthony Rouse.
This is a church centre, a worship area with associated facilities, built on the site of an earlier church by W.A. Pite. For its date, it is conservative, built of yellow brick with a steep roof and a very large side entrance in a transept. The interior is plain, but there a small circular window with stained glass above the altar.

Reference: Pevsner, 3, p. 123.

Other Churches

St Anne, Brondesbury

The former church by the Cutts brothers was demolished in 1996 and replaced by a circular building with extension: the Anglican section of this is the Trinity Chapel, about 12 feet by 12 feet and of great simplicity, incorporating some furnishings from the former church. Barbara Pym would weep.

Bromley

All Saints, Orpington
Status: in use.
Location: Bark Hart Road, north side.
Nearest station: Orpington.
Constructed: 1957–8.
Architect: Geddes Hyslop.
In Middlesex a number of small village churches remain, now mainly superseded
by newer buildings. At Greenford, a large new building was erected between the
wars next to the old church. Orpington grew very rapidly between the Wars,
but the question of church extension did not come to the fore until the 1950s.
The solution adopted here was to use the old church as the ante-chapel to a new
building three times larger, attached to it but orientated north/south, which was
designed along extremely traditional lines by Geddes Hyslop, who before the
War had been responsible for a far more radical project at the Bishop Andrewes
Church in St Helier. Here he built in late Gothic, of brick and flint, although
the piers and arches are of reinforced concrete, with aisles on both sides and five
projecting window bays. The interior has an equally anachronistic triptych behind
the altar, designed by Hyslop but painted by Brian Thomas. The overall result is a
very late flowering of the Gothic style which had so dominated church-building
for so long.

Reference: Pevsner, 2, pp. 188–9.

Christ Church, Anerley

Status: in use.
Location: Anerley Road, corner Maple Road.
Nearest station: Anerley.
Constructed: 1990.
Architect: Richard Watson & Partners.
This building is of bright red brick, low-built but with a small projecting lantern above the worship area. Externally, the composition is jumbled. Internally, the furnishings are clean and modern wood in the Evangelical style.

St Augustine, Bromley Common

Status: in use.

Location: Southborough Lane, north side, near junction with Homemead Road.

Nearest station: Petts Wood.

Constructed: 1957-8.

Architect: Victor Heal.

A tin tabernacle was erected for this area in 1913, and in 1938 local architect Victor Heal designed a hall. As early as 1943 it was decided that a new church was required but, as elsewhere, there was a prolonged gap before work could start. Heal volunteered to design the new building, on a more central site, and produced a substantial church, in light brick, which originally had a flat roof: in 1992 this was replaced by one with a shallow pitch after rain penetration. The building reflects an era of hope in the Church of England which was soon to end amid falling congregations. The lofty rectangular building has low ancillary areas attached, and a small bell-holder above. There are many plain glass windows. The interior is extremely traditional, with aisles on each side: the sanctuary, behind an arch, has a towering reredos as favoured by Victorians, with a small circular window above.

St Barnabas, St Paul's Cray

Status: in use.

Location: Rushet Road, east side, between junctions with Ravenscourt Road.

Nearest station: St Mary Cray.

Constructed: 1962-4.

Architect: E.F. Starling.

This area was developed after 1945 and a hut erected for worship in 1950. In 1953 a hall church was erected. It was established at an early stage that this was to be a firmly Evangelical ministry. Eventually a design was accepted which no doubt looked controversial at the time but has dated somewhat. The construction was problematic and the architect was dismissed in due course, before it was found that the roof leaked badly. The basic plan is cruciform, with very tall swooping roofs and a small spire above, which is a replacement for the original, which corroded. The roof dominates the interior also, with a network of exposed beams, and there is a very large window behind the holy table. There are galleries, an anachronistic feature, on three sides.

Reference: Pevsner, 2, p. 193.

St Edward the Confessor, Mottingham

Status: in use.
Location: St Keverne Road, opposite junction with Kimmeridge Road.
Nearest station: Mottingham.
Constructed: 1957.
Architect: D.E. Nye & Partners.

A hall church constructed in 1936 was regarded by the 1950s as insufficient for the needs of the developing estate, and in 1957 a substantial building was erected next to it. There is a large square tower at the west end, visually very powerful as the new church was erected in an open space. Behind it is a very traditional Gothic-influenced nave and chancel, with a number of arches across and many plain glass windows. There is a small exterior statue of the patron saint. The church is beautifully maintained.

St George RAF Chapel, Biggin Hill

Status: in use.

Location: Main Road, east side, north of junction with Saltbox Hill.

Nearest station: Orpington.

Constructed: 1951.

Architect: W. Wylton Todd.

This impressive memorial chapel is one of the relatively few post-1945 churches to be listed. It was constructed as early as 1951, to commemorate those who had died flying from Biggin Hill in the War, to replace an earlier chapel destroyed by fire. It is built in a loose Lombardic style with an unaisled nave and on the south side an oblong campanile. The chapel on the north side was a later addition. The furniture is spare, but Hugh Easton, the designer of the RAF memorial window in Westminster Abbey, designed a series of 12 windows each with the winged spirit of a young pilot holding a badge. The west window was added in 1981 and the four in the side chapel, by Goddard & Gibbs, in 1985. Although the RAF station is now closed, the chapel is open daily and has regular weekly services.

St Mark, Biggin Hill

Status: in use.
Location: Main Road, corner Church Road.
Nearest station: Orpington.
Constructed: 1957-9.
Architect: R. Gilbert Scott.

This is one of the more intriguing constructions of the time. The Biggin Hill area developed in the 1950s and the energetic vicar, the Revd Vivian Symons, wanted to replace the small iron church which had served the village since 1904. He did this by using much of the fabric of the church of All Saints, North Peckham, which was then being demolished, incorporating this into the new building designed by Scott. Thus while the completed building looks like a typical church of its era, it is full of imported Victorian details, not least the nave roof, which was rebuilt here as it was in Peckham. It is built of light brick, with very steeply pitched roof and a separate bell-tower. There is no east window, but a painted reredos on the wall. The indefatigable rector is commemorated by a brass: he constructed much himself, etched the windows and designed the altar plate and cross.

Reference: Pevsner, 2, p. 165.

St Mary, Shortlands

Status: in use.
Location: St Mary's Avenue, corner Kingswood Road.
Nearest station: Shortlands.
Constructed: 1953-5.
Architect: Arthur Bailey of Ansell & Bailey.
This church was bombed and was rebuilt on the same site: the result is a very typical product of post-war optimism, a tall rectangular light brick building with very large windows flooding the interior with light, but no spire. There is a particularly impressive neo-Perpendicular window in the east wall, which is externally surmounted by a relief of the flight from Egypt by John Skeaping. There are shallow arches dividing the nave from the aisles and the interior has contemporary furnishings pastel colourings on the walls.

References: Pevsner, 2, p. 194; SPWC, pp. 46-7.

St Mary of Nazareth, West Wickham

Status: in use.

Location: The Avenue, north side, west of junction with The Drive.

Nearest station: West Wickham.

Constructed: 1954.

Architect: C.W. Fowler.

This is a red-brick building with a large transept, neatly detailed but not original. There are large plain Gothic-style windows in each side of the aisleless nave and a relatively low roof with internal arches. There are a number of dated features, such as a separate baptistery and even an English altar with riddel posts. It replaced a hall designed by Martin Travers in 1934 and two plaques from the reredos in that hall, showing Our Lady and the Archangel Gabriel respectively, were incorporated into the new church in the lady chapel upstairs; both the chapel and the main altar have silver gilt wooden candlesticks, also apparently by Travers.

St Michael & All Angels, Beckenham

Status: in use.

Location: Ravenscroft Road, west side, south of junction with Avenue Road.

Nearest station: Avenue Road.

Constructed: 1955-6.

Architects: W.H. Hobday and F. J. Maynard.

The editors of Pevsner are very dismissive of this building, saying it is 'neo-Byzantine, of all things'. On the other hand, it has lasted well and is beautifully maintained. Unusually for a building of its age, it is strongly Anglo-Catholic in tradition, and has been furnished accordingly and provided with a multitude of stained glass windows from a variety of sources. It replaced a church damaged in the War. It is of light brick, towerless, and with an imposing west front with the door, topped by a tympanum, behind an arched portico. Internally it has aisles separated from the nave by low arches and some unfortunate visible trusses in the roof, which detract from the over all simplicity. There is a separate lady chapel.

Reference: Pevsner, 2, p. 159.

St Paul, Anerley

Status: in use.

Location: Hamlet Road, west side, near junction with Anerley Road.

Nearest station: Crystal Palace.

Constructed: 1977.

Architect: not known.

The unusual exterior appearance of this church belies its much more conventional interior. It is of grey brick with a lantern soaring above. This provides the light for the small octagonal worship area below, which is simply furnished, as the teaching is strongly Evangelical.

St Paul, Crofton

Status: in use.

Location: Crofton Lane, east side, south of junction with Beckford Drive.

Nearest station: Orpington.

Constructed: 1959.

Architect: A.B. Knapp-Fisher.

This church has more than a feel of Arts and Crafts architecture of 50 years before its construction, but unlike buildings of that era its elements do not hang together coherently. There is a squat wide tower leading to a nave with a steeply graded barrel roof broken by areas of flat roof and by dormer windows which rather oddly run right down to the ground. There are rose windows in both east and west walls, that over the altar being filled with abstract stained glass. There are narrow passage aisles on each side. The over all effect is not unpleasant, but is strongly retrospective. It replaced a hall church which is still used as a hall.

Reference: Pevsner, 2, p. 189.

St Peter & St Paul, Bromley

Status: in use.

Location: Church Road, south side.

Nearest station: Bromley North.

Reconstructed: 1957.

Architect: J. Harold Gibbons.

This church was damaged in the air raids which hit Bromley in 1941. It was rebuilt under the direction of Gibbons, who had designed a number of distinguished churches in London and elsewhere between the Wars. This is not one of his more original designs, not least because he adapted to the continued existence of the tower. He built here in a Gothic-derived style, with nave and chancel under one roof, a chapel with apse and a prominent transept.

Reference: Pevsner, 2, p. 166.

Other Churches

Church of Unity, Orpington
A united Anglican-Methodist church was constructed in 1967 in Rye Crescent. It is a hall with a simple sanctuary which can be curtained off. Externally, it resembles a poor primary school.

St Mark, Bromley
The church of 1897-8 by Evelyn Hellicar, son of the vicar, was badly bombed. The tower and the nave arcades were incorporated into a rebuilt church by D.E. Nye & Partners in 1953, apparently to designs by T.F.W. Grant, with transverse arches.

St Nicholas, Farnborough

In 1957-8 a prefabricated building was erected in Leamington Avenue, which was intended to be temporary but has proved not to be so. It is a low building with barrel roof.

Camden

Holy Trinity, Swiss Cottage

Status: in use.

Location: Finchley Road, opposite tube station of that name.

Nearest station: Finchley Road.

Constructed: 1978.

Architect: Biscoe & Stanton.

This replacement for a Victorian church is a low multi-cornered dark brick building with a wrap around wall encompassing an entrance area: there is a lantern above. The interior is almost entirely bare with the altar pushed into the corner to make way for the drums and guitars.

Reference: Pevsner, 4, p. 201.

St Cuthbert, West Hampstead

Status: in use.

Location: Fordwych Road, east side, opposite St Cuthbert's Road.

Nearest station: Kilburn.

Constructed: 1987-8.

Architect: Jeremy Allen.

This church replaced a late Victorian building, some of the site of which was used for flats. It is very different: it is designed to be welcoming and externally is somewhat unobtrusive, although well thought out. It is polygonal, with lighting from above and from windows on either side of the sanctuary, and a high wooden ceiling. There is little furniture, the worship being firmly Evangelical, but behind the holy table are two reset panels from a stained glass window from the old building (the Raising of Lazarus by Henry Holiday) and immediately in front of the entrance is a bell from that church on a circular plinth.

Reference: Pevsner, 4, p. 201.

Other Churches

St Paul, Camden Square

A hall of about 1950 with a worship area at the east end, featuring an unexpected stained glass window, is still in use as a temporary replacement for a church bombed in the War. Various schemes for redevelopment have been floated.

City of London

St Andrew, Holborn

Status: in use.

Location: St Andrew Street, by Holborn Circus.

Nearest station: Chancery Lane.

Reconstructed: 1960.

Architect: Seely & Paget.

It was decided in the case of this church that it should be restored as it had been before the bombing which destroyed it. The sympathetic practice of Seely & Paget was an appropriate designer for this: for example they made a new reredos to reproduce that which it had had before. There is a great deal of glass by Brian Thomas.

References: Pevsner, 1, pp. 190–1; Clarke, p. 41.

St Ethelburga, Bishopsgate

Status: now used as a Centre for Reconciliation and Peace.
Location: Bishopsgate, east side, south of junction with Camomile Street.
Nearest station: Liverpool Street.
Reconstructed: 1998.
Architects: Purcell Miller Tritton.
After being severely damaged by an IRA bomb in 1993, this, the smallest church
in the City, was reconstructed to its original plan, and even the narrow front
was rebuilt in an approximation of what was there before. The interior was
much altered for its new role, incorporating those few fittings which survived,
including a parclose screen by Comper.

Reference: Pevsner, 1, pp. 218-19.

St Vedast, Foster Lane

Status: in use.

Location: Foster Lane, east side, north of junction with Cheapside.

Nearest station: St Paul's.

Reconstructed: 1953-62.

Architect: S.E. Dykes-Bower.

This church was very badly damaged in the War and virtually all the furnishings were lost. It is remarkable in that the architect of the rebuilding was Stephen Dykes-Bower, who was able to recreate a suitable interior for the Wren building, not least because he was able to reuse a variety of items which had been rescued from other contemporary churches. The wood which was used was dark-stained so as to appear one. The ceiling was reinstalled and decorated and new stained glass by Brian Thomas was installed in the east wall. It is a remarkable restoration which owes almost nothing to the twentieth century.

References: Pevsner, 1, pp. 265-6; Clarke, p. 43; A. Symondson, *Stephen Dykes-Bower*, London, 2011, pp. 32-5.

Other Churches

A very large number of City churches were substantially rebuilt in post-war years because of damage suffered. In this volume we have selected three of particular interest, two of which were reconstructed after the War and one after being bombed. The work carried out to the others, although fascinating, has little relevance to the building of new churches in the period covered by this book.

Croydon

All Saints, Spring Park

Status: in use.

Location: Bridle Road, corner Farm Drive.

Nearest station: West Wickham.

Constructed: 1956.

Architect: Curtis Green, Son & Lloyd.

This is a classic 1950s, ultra-traditional church, of a design which soon became obsolete. It is built of light brick with a squat tower with belfry above the chancel. There are tall transepts on each side and late Gothic arches supporting the roof at the crossing. There is also a separate lady chapel. The interior is white and the high walls inside accentuate the contemporary furnishings. This is a church which critics will deride, but fifty years on it has mellowed and has acquired a certain timelessness.

Christ Church, Croydon

Status: in use.
Location: Sumner Road, corner Longley Road.
Nearest station: West Croydon.
Constructed: 1991.
Architect: Maurice Taylor.

This replaced a church of 1851-2 by Teulon, which was closed in 1978 and damaged by fire in 1985. Three bays at the west end and the chancel remained, and were incorporated into the new building, the hall in the west end. The new red brick worship area was built on and is of little architectural importance. The worship is Evangelical.

St Antony, Sanderstead

Status: in use.

Location: Wentworth Way, near junction with Clyde Avenue.

Nearest station: Upper Warlingham.

Constructed: 1957.

Architect: A.W. Kenyon.

In Hamsey Green, on the very outskirts of Greater London, this was one of the first hall/churches, which has remained largely as built. There is a stage at the west end and a chancel at the east, with a sliding screen which can be opened for services. It is a tall light brick building with shallow pitched roof and high windows on each side of the hall. The sanctuary arrangements are typical of the age, with a tall crucifix hung behind the altar.

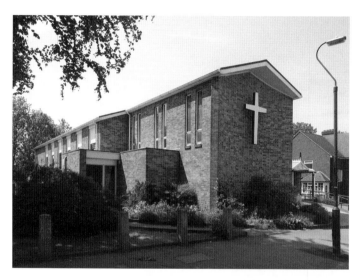

St Barnabas, Purley

Status: in use.
Location: Higher Drive, opposite Bencombe Road.
Nearest station: Reedham.
Constructed: 1959.
Architects: George Lowe & Partners.
This church was by local architects on a hill site, and incorporates a hall and other rooms. It is a curious creation of its time, externally resembling a secular building, with copper roofing, and of no great distinction inside, save for a painting of the Madonna and Child by John Hayward.

St Edmund, Riddlesdown

Status: in use.

Location: Mitchley Avenue, north side, east of Lower Bar Road.

Nearest station: Riddlesdown.

Constructed: 1955.

Architect: not known.

This is another early hall/church: it was built by Laings the builders as part of the development of the area, replacing a temporary building. As early as 1965 it was proposed that it be replaced by a larger church, but this proposal was never taken forward. It has a somewhat confused external profile, built of light brick with shallow roofs, but internally it has quite an elaborate sanctuary and some interesting windows

St Edward King & Confessor, New Addington

Status: in use.
Location: Central Parade, far end.
Nearest station: New Addington.
Constructed: 1958.
Architects: Caroe & Partners.

To serve the vast new town of New Addington, this church, described by the editors of Pevsner as 'red brick, conservative and uninspiring', was provided, to replace a temporary building. That conventional reproach underestimates the strength of the design, admittedly traditional. It has a low nave, chancel and two transepts of light brick with a separate chapel behind the chancel, separated by a wooden screen. There is a belfry over the entrance, and a number of stained glass windows. There is a chapel of St George, to whom other buildings on the estate have been dedicated.

Reference: Pevsner, 2, p. 205.

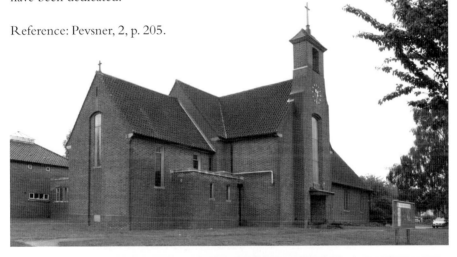

St George, Shirley
Status: in use.
Location: The Grade, corner Elstan Way.
Nearest station: Arena.
Constructed: 1952.
Architect: John L. Denman.
This was an early construction after the War and could perhaps be called unusual: it is of red brick, and the prominent tower has peaked walls surmounted by a copper towerlet. There are rows of windows on each side of the nave. There is an aisle on the south side only, and flat roofed ancillary rooms, some added in 1960, around the sanctuary. There are false ceilings in the nave and sanctuary of plaster on hessian stretched over a wooden frame. There is a gallery above the east end and running around. This is not the most successful design of the era.

St John the Evangelist, Old Coulsdon

Status: in use.
Location: Canons Hill, east side, on Church Path.
Nearest station: Coulsdon South.
Constructed: 1958.
Architect: J.B.S. Comper.

This is an interesting application of Gothic work at a very late date. By the late 1950s the old parish church of the village of Old Coulsdon was far too small for the developing area. It was decided that instead of building a completely new building, the south wall of the mediaeval building would be demolished and Sebastian Comper was invited to design a very traditional extension leading out from the existing nave. The new area is much larger than the old. It can be screened off along the line of the former south wall, enabling either section to be used separately. Comper designed in a Decorated style, with an altar in the chancel with a baldachino above, elevated by three steps.

Reference: Pevsner, 2, p. 206.

St Matthew, Croydon

Status: in use.

Location: Chichester Road, north side, corner Park Hill.

Nearest station: East Croydon.

Constructed: 1965-72.

Architect: David Bush.

This church, built for the developing Park Hill Estate, represents new trends which were becoming apparent at that time and which are reflected also in the architect's other building in Peckham. It is a substantially-sized hexagon with solid brick walls: the light comes from above, through vertical glazing which separates the many roof levels: in addition there is a tall aluminium-clad tower, which adds yet another dimension visually. There is a central foyer off which the church and all ancillary rooms lead. There is stained glass from the former St Matthew, George Street, by John Hayward.

Reference: Pevsner, 2, p. 210.

St Swithun, Purley

Status: in use.
Location: Grovelands Road, corner Downlands Road.
Nearest station: Reedham.
Constructed: 1954.
Architects: D.E. Nye & Partners.

This is an unusual building which was planned and partly built before the War under the 25 Churches scheme, to replace a hall, to a design by Cachemaille-Day. The walls which had been started before the War were demolished, and a new church constructed by D.E. Nye & Partners, finally opening in 1954. It is built in a striking position on a steep slope, which gives it great visual presence, although there is no tower. The building was designed on traditional lines, with a five-sided apse at the east end and many internal arches. There is a gallery at the west end with a plaque of the nativity, and a stained glass window commemorating St Peter, Greenwich, and Holy Trinity, Blackheath, destroyed in the War: from the proceeds of the sites, this church was financed.

Reference: SPWC, p. 38, K. Richardson, *The 'Twenty-Five' Churches of the Southwark Diocese*, London, 2002, pp. 110-12.

Other Churches

St Francis, Selsdon

A small mission church was designed by Northover & Northover in 1962 in Tedder Road. A small belfry is the only distinguishing feature externally and internally it is a conventional hall/church.

St George, New Addington

A mission church was built for the Castle Hill area in 1962, but it was burned out in 1983 and the site later cleared.

Ealing

All Saints, South Acton

Status: in use.

Location: Bollo Bridge Road, south side, opposite Newton Avenue.

Nearest station: South Acton.

Constructed: 1985.

Architect: A.J. Monk

This church centre was built to replace a Victorian church. It presents almost unbroken brick walls to the outside wall, but with a stylized belfry above and a semi-circle between the two visible walls.

Christ the Redeemer, Southall

Status: in use.

Location: Allenby Road, between Bycroft Road and Sunnycroft Road.

Nearest station: Greenford.

Constructed: 1964.

Architect: Michael Farey.

This is one of the relatively few churches which was consciously modelled
on the work of the New Churches Research Group. Michael Farey designed
a building to reflect the ideas of the incumbent, the Revd George Grainger,
namely that it should not look like a church, but rather should be a building for
the performance of the liturgy. There is a circular area with a bell cage above in
the centre of the building, between the church and the hall. The church, to the
north, is a simple brick structure but has 28 small coloured windows in a pattern
on the wall by the road and a large window above the entrance. The stained glass
in the lantern is by Trahearne.

Reference: Pevsner, 3, p. 192.

Emmanuel, Southall

Status: in use.
Location: Fleming Road, corner Osborne Road.
Nearest station: Hanwell.
Constructed: 1974.
Architect: Richard Pratley.
This is a small square dual purpose hall/church which is strongly Evangelical in tone. It has a curved corner for the sanctuary, which is characteristically bare.

Reference: Pevsner, 3, p. 192.

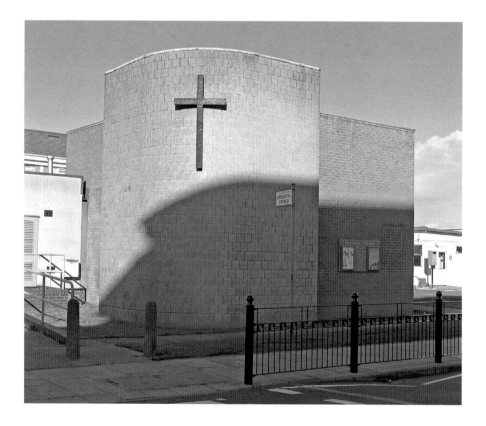

St Christopher, Hanwell

Status: in use.
Location: Bordars Road, north side, east of Hillyard Road.
Nearest station: Castle Bar Park.
Constructed: 2003.
Architect: not known.

This striking building was the result of a unique collaboration between
the Diocese of London and the YMCA. The site of the former church was
redeveloped with a smaller new church and a 40-bed hostel run by the charity.
The church is of yellow brick with a steeply pitched roof and three long clear
windows in the geographically south wall, which throw light on the sanctuary.

St Hugh of Lincoln, Northolt

Status: in use.

Location: Kensington Road, east side, north of Ruislip Road.

Nearest station: Northolt.

Constructed: 1970.

Architect: I. Nellist.

This is a low brick building of no great architectural distinction but with some stained glass behind the altar.

Reference: Pevsner, 3, p. 187 (where it is wrongly said to be a Roman Catholic church).

St Joseph the Worker, Northolt

Status: in use.

Location: Radcliffe Way, near junction with Yeading Lane.

Nearest station: Northolt.

Constructed: 1967.

Architects: Maguire & Murray.

The less well-known of Maguire & Murray's two London churches and built well after St Paul, Bow Common, St Joseph, Northolt, has a common commitment to the Liturgical Movement. Externally there is a striking free-standingconcrete campanile tower, almost on the pavement. The church itself is rectangular, the upper part covered in zinc, and the cynic would say it resembled a fortress. The interior is spacious and high, with curious thin columns leading up to the roof, those on either side of the altar being joined as if ladders, and is painted white throughout. It appears that it was designed with reference to the factories in which many of the parishioners worked. Against that background the contemporary furnishings stand out. There was a separate baptistery, slightly below the level of the main church, now made into a coffee lounge.

References: Pevsner, 3, p. 186; G. Adler: *Robert Maguire & Keith Murray*, London, 2012, pp. 93-6.

St Mary & St Nicholas, Perivale

Status: in use.

Location: Federal Road, opposite corner with Wadsworth Road.

Nearest station: Perivale.

Constructed: 1963.

Architect: Laurence King.

This is one of the few churches which owes a considerable debt to Maguire & Murray's pioneering building in Bow Common, in that it is centrally planned and the altar is lit from above. It is of red brick with extensive copper coverings on the roofs. However, Laurence King was a more conventional architect and the design has lasted well. The church, like its designer, had Anglo-Catholic inspiration and a large corona and rood together with other furnishings were installed.

Reference: Pevsner, 3, p. 190.

St Mary, West Twyford

Status: in use.
Location: Brentmead Gardens, east side.
Nearest station: Park Royal.
Constructed: 1958.
Architect: N.F. Cachemaille-Day.

One of Cachemaille-Day's later churches was built in this little-known corner of London, and incorporated a small chapel rebuilt in the early nineteenth century. Of yellow brick, the church is of substantial size for its date, and has a square tower with windows set in concrete frames and a statue of Our Lady over the door: the tall nave has windows, many set high in it, and external brick pillars. The east window is contemporary, by A.E. Buss, and the west wall has a number of small windows. The interior has unusual columns which taper outwards towards the roof. For a time this modern church was derelict inside and worship continued in the hall next door which had been used as the church before 1958. It has now been listed, restored externally, and cleared and is used again: the hall is leased to the Seventh Day Adventists.

Reference: Pevsner, 3, pp. 197–8.

St Richard, Northolt

Status: in use.

Location: Sussex Crescent at corner with Southwell Avenue.

Nearest station: Northolt.

Constructed: 1960.

Architect: not known.

This is a small and unpretentious brick hall church, which has been altered since it was constructed so that the original church is now the hall and the rather limited worship area is at right angles to the original. It does have a statue of the patron saint, an unusual dedication.

Other Churches

St Stephen, West Ealing

The Victorian church has been converted into flats and worshippers now use the old church hall, to which was added in 1986 a rectangular brick complex with pagoda-like roof, lit by a clerestory: it was designed by I. Goldsmid.

Enfield

St Alphege, Edmonton

Status: in use.
Location: Hertford Road, west side, opposite Nightingale Road.
Nearest station: Southbury.
Constructed: 1957-8.
Architect: Edward Maufe.
As is to be expected from the distinguished architect who designed it, this is a church of considerable merit. Maufe lived until 1974 and this is one of his last ecclesiastical productions. It could be described as having a quiet, understated authority. It is built of pale brick with a conventional roof and has external statues of the Crucifixion, against the window on the east wall, and of St Alphege, on the narrow west bell-tower. The liturgical setting is traditional, with a long nave and an elevated sanctuary with a striking painting of the Crucifixion by C. Pearson behind the later. There are aisles on both sides, beneath tall clear windows. The tradition is Anglo-Catholic.

Reference: Pevsner, 4, p. 423.

St Mary, Lower Edmonton

Status: now used as youth centre and pre-school by local authority.
Location: Lawrence Road corner Baxter Road.
Nearest station: Silver Street.
Constructed: 1970.
Architect: Brian Freebourne.
A large church by Butterfield, built in 1883, was demolished in 1957 and replaced by a small modern building, which has now been leased by the local authority for secular use. It is of pale brick, flat roofed, and marked out only by a strange exterior sculpture. The tiny worship area was plain.

Reference: Pevsner, 4, p. 424.

St Michael-at-Bowes, Wood Green

Status: in use.

Location: Palmerston Road corner Whittington Road.

Nearest station: Bowes Park.

Constructed: 1987–8.

Architect: not known.

This is yet another parish where the Victorian church (by G.G. Scott) was demolished, in this case in 1987, and replaced on a new site by a smaller building which is easier to heat and light. Externally it is marked by a low steeply sloping roof from which projects a dormer with a statue of St Michael on it. The projection lights the altar and there are further windows at the top of the west wall. The interesting aspect of this re-creation is that the alabaster altarpiece was reused and the marble reredos was split and used to make a new altar, lectern, font and credence table. A powerful new crucifix by Francis Stephens hangs behind the altar and there are also new statues of St Michael and the Blessed Virgin by Siegfried Pietsch.

Reference: Pevsner, 4, p. 455.

St Peter & St Paul, Enfield Lock

Status: in use.

Location: Ordnance Road, corner Chesterfield Road.

Nearest station: Enfield Lock.

Constructed: 1969.

Architect: R.B. Craze.

The church constructed here in 1928 was demolished by a bomb in 1944 but not replaced until 1969. Romilly Craze was generally a safe pair of hands when it came to designing suburban churches: however, his building here was rather odd. The pale brick and long nave are entirely conventional, but the church has a very long apse projecting from the west end and a curious attenuated tower over the entrance, with a smaller stage above. The church has always had an Anglo-Catholic tradition.

Reference: Pevsner, 4, p. 438.

Other Churches

St Giles, Enfield

A substantial church was erected in Bullsmoor Lane in 1953-4, to the design of J. Barrington Baker & Partners. It was an early hall/church with the worship area divided from the main hall by a folding screen. The building was barn-shaped and of no great distinction. It has been demolished.

Greenwich

All Saints, Shooters Hill

Status: in use.

Location: Ripon Road, corner Herbert Terrace.

Nearest station: Woolwich Arsenal.

Constructed: 1956-7.

Architect: Thomas F. Ford.

The churches of Thomas Ford deserve more credit than they are customarily given. Here, as elsewhere in the Diocese of Southwark, he produced a new church of some distinction. It replaced a building of 1944 which was bombed. It is of brick with a pitched roof and a tower with octagonal top section. Pevsner says that he used 'primly eclectic details': certainly the sources are varied, but the design, albeit conservative in form, works well. The furnishings are good and contemporary and as with other churches of its era there is a Feibusch mural behind the altar. The usual predominant white colour scheme is relieved by a bright turquoise but that runs as a theme and thus looks better than it sounds. There are a large number of clear windows.

References: Pevsner, 2, p. 279; Clarke, p. 257.

St Alban, Mottingham

Status: in use.

Location: William Barefoot Drive, corner Southold Rise.

Nearest station: New Eltham.

Constructed: 1955-6.

Architect: Ralph Covell.

This is a building which can perhaps now be given more appreciation that was the case when it was constructed in a then new housing area. It is a simple but well-executed design with a barrel roof and a tower and with largely contemporary furnishings: on the same site are the vicarage and the hall, also barrel-roofed, which can be opened out into the church itself. Internally there is a dignified sanctuary with an unusual stained glass window (by W. Carter Shapland) behind the altar and bowed outwards. There are other clear windows on both sides of the nave.

Reference: SPWC, pp. 66-7.

St Francis, Eltham

Status: now a community centre.

Location: Sibthorpe Road, corner Hengist Road.

Nearest station: Lee.

Constructed: 1953.

Architect: Ralph Covell.

This is a simple barrel-roofed brick building, with arches to the entrance area, a single small bell, and, most distinctively, a seven-light stained glass window in somewhat lurid colours. It has a chequered history: it was originally within the parish of St John, Eltham, and was used regularly as a mission church until 1962: there appears to have been a temporary predecessor for a few years before this building was constructed. In 1981 the parish leased it to the Horn Park Community Association but after the expiry of the lease in 2006 it was again used for occasional services, this time by the parish of St Saviour, Eltham, into which the area had been transferred. It now appears to be used solely for secular purposes.

Reference: SPWC, pp. 100–1.

St John, Plumstead

Status: in use.

Location: Earl Rise, corner Robert Street.

Nearest station: Plumstead.

Constructed: 1959.

Architect: not known.

This is a small brick-built church which was constructed on the site of a Victorian church which was bombed: it uses parts of the transept and chancel walls which remained standing. Part of the former nave was transformed into a church hall and two extensions have been added to the main building. There is a pitched roof but a barrel ceiling within. Internally, the furnishings are simple, the teaching being Conservative Evangelical, and there is little decoration save for a window depicting the Good Shepherd and a reredos, presumably from the former church.

St Mark & St Margaret, Plumstead

Status: in use.

Location: Old Mill Road, corner Chestnut Rise.

Nearest station: Plumstead.

Constructed: 1976.

Architect: David Bush.

This church replaced the two parish churches whose dedications it took. St Margaret was demolished in the 1960s and St Mark, which had been constructed in the Romanesque style as recently as 1901, in 1974. Some furnishings from the latter were incorporated into the much smaller new building, which also has offices and the like attached. The chancel is square in shape and can be shut off from the main seated area. There is an odd entrance lobby which stands up above the rest of the buildings but the entire composition is unprepossessing. It has a number of stained glass windows from the former church.

Reference: Pevsner, 2, p. 280.

St Nicholas, Kidbrooke

Status: in use.
Location: Whetstone Road, south side, between Holburne and Hapgood Roads.
Nearest station: Kidbrooke.
Constructed: 1953.
Architect: not known.

This was one of the first buildings built after the War in order to provide for an expanding area of population: it reused the dedication of the mediaeval church in Kidbrooke, which had fallen into ruin many years before. It replaced a hut. The money was raised by house to house collections locally and provided not only for the church but the adjoining hall. It demonstrates well that at that time it was not regarded as acceptable to combine the two. It is a plain but appealing rectangular brick building with pitched roof and vaulted ceiling. Most of the windows are clear but it does have two of stained glass. It has a small bellcote with louvred sides. Over the altar is a mural of St Nicholas painted by Hugh Powell at the time the church was constructed, which has a naïve charm. Some other features have been bought in over the years, such as the organ, acquired from the Royal Herbert Military Hospital in 1978, and a seventeenth-century bell from St Mark, Bromley.

St Paul, Thamesmead

Status: in use.

Location: Bentham Road, east side, near junction with Oriole Way.

Nearest station: Abbey Wood.

Constructed: 1976-8.

Architect: Hinton, Brown, Maddon & Langstone.

In the new Thamesmead area the churches combined so that one building could be used by Anglicans, Romans, Methodists, and the URC. There are two churches under one roof, the first for the Roman Catholics and the second for the three other participants, but they can be opened out into each other. It is a low brick-built single-storey building with a central section which is much higher and presents a plain wall to the outside. The most distinctive feature was a delicate free-standing corona in metal, which has now been removed. Internally there are some primitive paintings and a number of windows designed by children.

Reference: Pevsner, 2, p. 299.

St Peter, Lee

Status: in use.

Location: Eltham Road, corner Weigall Road.

Nearest station: Lee.

Constructed: 1983.

Architect: not known.

There have been no fewer than three churches of St Peter, Lee. The first, a Victorian building nearby, was closed just before the Second World War because of a declining congregation. It was later demolished but demand grew again, and in 1960 N.F. Cachemaille-Day designed a new church on the present site. This seems to be little remembered. It suffered from subsidence and after barely more than twenty years was itself demolished and replaced by the present building, which is small and unobtrusive and in the dual-purpose mode which had become fashionable. The only distinctive feature is a semi-circular projection from the building.

William Temple Church, Abbey Wood

Status: in use.

Location: Eynsham Road, north side, between Finchale and Penmon Roads.

Nearest station: Abbey Wood.

Constructed: 1966.

Architect: not known.

This church is very much of its age and reflects a design for a moderate Anglo-Catholic parish. It is square, with the entrance and the sanctuary at opposing corners. Clear windows run all the way round above the side walls and there is a timber-built pyramidal roof with a copper-coated flèche above. The sanctuary fittings now begin to look dated, particularly the circular area around the altar with communion rails, and the wooden dossal behind the altar. Even at the date of construction, although the altar was designed for westward position, it was not placed centrally, as it could easily have been.

Other Churches

Christ Church, East Greenwich

In 1989 , following the redundancy of the Victorian church in Trafalgar Road, a new smaller church was constructed around and partly within the fabric, designed by John Brown and Robert Kerr.

Church of the Cross, Thamesmead

In Lensbury Way a small single storey flat roofed building was constructed in 1975 as a shared church with ancillary accommodation attached. A large cross in the grass outside is the only indication of its purpose.

Holy Spirit, Kidbrooke

In about 1971 a shop/church was opened in Teleman Square on the Ferrier Estate. Externally it differs little from commercial premises, save that it has on the façade a gaudy stained glass window.

St Mary, Charlton

A small community centre and chapel was built in Charlton Park Lane in 1961 to designs by Ralph Covell. It had a steep roof with five triangular dormer windows on each side and a small open metalwork spire above. It suffered badly from subsidence, closed in 1974 and was demolished shortly thereafter.

Hackney

Risen Christ & All Souls, Clapton Park

Status: in use.

Location: Overbury Street, near junction with Rushmore Raod.

Nearest station: Homerton.

Constructed: 1977.

Architect: Freddie To.

This building replaced the Victorian church of All Souls, which had a notable Anglo-Catholic tradition. Externally it is unobtrusive, with only a cross in the red brick wall proclaiming its presence. It has a low flat roof with a slightly raised area in the centre, which provides light through clerestory windows for the plain worship area beneath. Inside the windows are galleries with plants growing. The church is designed so that the wooden altar table is on one of the longer walls: the tradition of the worship has disappeared.

St John the Evangelist, Brownswood Park

Status: in use.
Location: Gloucester Drive corner Queens Drive.
Nearest station: Finsbury Park.
Constructed: 1995.
Architect: Tom Hornsby.

This is a replacement of a very substantial Venetian-style Victorian church: some of the windows have been incorporated into the new building. The design is ingenious and eye-catching: one end of the building is semi-circular, with ancillary rooms around the sanctuary and above is a large circular lantern, which provides even more light than floods in from the clerestory below. The sanctuary is thus placed traditionally, rather than centrally, and is slightly elevated. All the furniture is plain wood. This is a more ambitious and successful building than many of its time.

St Michael & All Angels, London Fields

Status: in use.

Location: Lansdowne Drive, corner Lavender Grove.

Nearest station: London Fields.

Constructed: 1959-61.

Architect: N.F. Cachemaille-Day.

Cachemaille-Day constructed this church shortly after completing nearby St Paul's, but here his approach was very different. The building also includes a great deal of work by John Hayward, and the combination of the two has led to it being listed. The building is square with the altar placed centrally beneath a concrete dome covered in copper. Around the altar is a wooden corona, supported not from above but by piers, also wooden. This too was designed by the architect and was intended to represent the Crown of Thorns. Cachemaille-Day also designed the clerestory windows, including one of St Michael. John Hayward, best known himself for his glass, produced the apostles' windows on the east side, nine distinctive murals, and a powerful aluminium statue of St Michael slaying the dragon, which is hung over the door and has recently been restored. The entire building was designed and furnished together and this is an unusual and valuable feature.

References: Pevsner, 4, p. 483; Clarke, p. 71.

St Paul, West Hackney

Status: in use.

Location: Stoke Newington Road, between Amhurst and Evering Roads.

Nearest station: Rectory Road.

Constructed: 1958-60.

Architect: N.F. Cachemaille-Day.

This replaced a bombed church of 1821-4 by Smirke. Cachemaille-Day displays his talent here, albeit in a setting where economy was important. It is a rectangle with windows only on the south and west sides (liturgically), built of pale brick with concrete frames visible inside. There are no aisles or side chapels, and no separate chancel, although the altar is set forward with communion rails around it: the hall is separate rather than combined. There are interesting furnishings, including a corona above the sanctuary, a fine west window of the conversion of St Paul by John Hayward, small windows of the symbols of the Evangelists by Goddard & Gibbs, and wall paintings by Christopher Webb, including a fine Christ in Glory on the east wall.

References: Pevsner, 4, pp. 483-4; Clarke, p. 70.

Other Churches

Christ Church on the Mead, Homerton

This is the Wally Foster community centre in Homerton Road, built about 1970, which contains within it a small room fitted out for worship in a fairly primitive way.

Hammersmith & Fulham

St Clement, Fulham

Status: in use.

Location: Fulham Palace Road, near corner Niton Street.

Nearest station: Hammersmith.

Constructed: 1975-6.

Architect: Biscoe & Stanton.

The former Victorian church of 1885-6, by Blomfield, was demolished about 1969 and replaced by flats and a small church centre. It is a hall with a wrap round wall towards the road with a large cross on it, and the chancel is lit from above: there is an upward projection covered in copper. There are a number of items, such as a war memorial, from the former church.

Reference: Pevsner, 3, p. 232.

St Etheldreda, Fulham

Status: in use.
Location: Fulham Palace Road, corner Doneraile Street.
Nearest station: Putney Bridge.
Constructed: 1955-8.
Architect: Guy Biscoe.

The former Victorian church was demolished and replaced by a plain, barn-like structure with an almost unbroken brick wall on the north or road side. Its most prominent feature is a rectangular north-east tower with a belfry. There is also a low semi-circular baptistery emerging from the west wall with a series of tall stained glass windows by W. Carter Shapland. Internally, the concrete portal frame is apparent, and there is a shallow sanctuary with a large carved crucifix, by Rita Ling, over the altar and windows in the side.

References: Pevsner, 3, pp. 232-3; Clarke, p. 62.

St Katherine, East Acton
Status: in use.
Location: Westway, corner Primula Street.
Nearest station: East Acton.
Constructed: 1958.
Architect: J.R. Atkinson.
This church is built on the foundations of the church of St Katherine Coleman, constructed in 1922 and designed by the architect's father. It was destroyed in the War. It took its dedication from a demolished City church, the only relic of which is the communion rails in a chapel. The outline of the new church is similar to the old, save for the omission of the apse, but the construction is completely different. There are no side windows and the framing is of steel, with the piers between brick areas on the sides. There are fittings which were mostly added after construction, and in 1975 part of the west end was divided off.

References: Pevsner, p. 204; Clarke, p. 76.

St Luke, Shepherd's Bush

Status: in use.
Location: Uxbridge Road, corner Wormholt Street.
Nearest station: Shepherd's Bush Market.
Constructed: 1976–8.
Architect: A.J. Monk.

A church of 1871–2 was demolished and replaced by this striking but small red brick building, a vicarage, and flats. John Hayward provided an east window using glass from the former church. There is a bell tower at the west end which consists of two thin piers, and at the east end the roof over the chancel rises up in correspondence. There is also a round baptistery. From the outside the appearance is distinctly fractured, but internally it looks much more conventional. There is a strong Anglo-Catholic tradition.

Reference: Pevsner, 3, p. 204.

St Mary, West Kensington

Status: in use.

Location: Edith Road, corner Hammersmith Road.

Nearest station: Barons Court.

Constructed: 1960-1.

Architects: Seely & Paget.

This was originally a chapel, built in 1814, which was substantially enlarged in 1883-4. In 1960-1 Seely & Paget completely rebuilt it, albeit in a very conservative style and one fitted for the Evangelical worship which had always been maintained here. The church is now long and rectangular, with aisles at a lower level on each side and clerestory windows above. There is a tower with a narrow copper spire and an unusual entrance area with portico. Inside is equally traditional: there are round-headed arches and this motif is carried forward into the ceiling and the east wall, which has three arches and a small rose window behind the holy table.

References: Pevsner, 3, p. 233; Clarke, pp. 62-3.

St Michael & St George, White City

Status: in use.
Location: Commonwealth Avenue, corner Canada Way.
Nearest station: White City.
Constructed: 1952.
Architects: Seely & Paget.
This is a very early post-war construction, an unpretentious but pleasing low brick building with curved roofs. Inside, there are contemporary furnishings including a wall painting by Brian Thomas. The altar is a striking edifice of stone which was given very old-fashioned looking fittings behind and a large Christus Rex, replacing a mural by Brian Thomas.

References: Pevsner, 3, p. 204; SPWC, pp. 104-5.

Haringey

Christ Church, West Green

Status: in use.

Location: Waldeck Road, between Carlingford and Stanmore Roads.

Nearest station: Turnpike Lane.

Constructed: 1982.

Architects: Riley & Glanfield.

This replaced a Victorian church: it is an unpretentious brown brick building with shallow pitched roofs and a startling large dormer window over the entrance filled with bright glass. There is a lantern over the east end which lights the sanctuary and aisles on both sides, the south containing a chapel. There is a large statue of Christ the King on the east wall above an ornately decorated tabernacle. The church is strongly Anglo-Catholic and there are a number of statues and a banner of Our Lady of Fatima.

Reference: Pevsner, 4, p. 571.

Good Shepherd, Wood Green
Status: sold to and used by Eritrean Christians.
Location: Stirling Road, corner Berwick Road.
Nearest station: Wood Green.
Constructed: 1961.
Architect: not known.
In 1916 a corrugated iron and wood church was moved here from Neasden, and was then used as a mission of St Michael, Wood Green. There was a separate hall. The building deteriorated and following a fund-raising campaign and the sale off of the hall, a small pale brick, rather crude dual-purpose building was erected in 1961. However, as with other places, it had a very short life and as numbers fell it was closed and then sold to Eritreans.

St Andrew, Alexandra Park

Status: in use.

Location: Alexandra Park Road, corner Windermere Road.

Nearest station: Alexandra Palace.

Reconstructed: 1957.

Architect: Randall S. Morris.

This church, by Alder (1903), was gutted in the War, but the north, south and east walls were incorporated into the reconstruction by Morris in 1957 in conventional form. He built a new west wall with large window and a semicircular entrance area beneath: the nave was given a clerestory with octagonal stone piers and brick arches. There is a belfry above. The overall impression is of a church built perhaps 80 years before.

Reference: Pevsner, 4, p. 550.

St Mary with St George, Hornsey

Status: in use.

Location: Cranley Gardens, north side, near junction with Park Road.

Nearest station: Highgate.

Constructed: 1959.

Architect: Randall S. Morris.

This church was constructed to replace the bombed St George and was later joined by those who attended St Mary, Hornsey Parish Church. It is a distinctive and well-crafted traditional building in pale brick, which makes particular use of high arches: these are found internally, supporting the steeply graded roof, and in the east and west windows. There is a prominent bell tower on the north-west corner.

Reference: Pevsner, 4, p. 551.

St Paul, Harringay

Status: in use.

Location: Wightman Road, corner Burgoyne Road.

Nearest station: Harringay.

Constructed: 1988–93.

Architect: Peter Jenkins.

This is in visual impact one of the most remarkable modern churches in London: further it was provided with a set of high-quality contemporary furnishings. It was constructed to replace an earlier building destroyed by fire in 1984. Externally, it appears as a bright red brick windowless rectangle surmounted by a very steeply graded roof which projects front and back in a strong triangle with glazed centre. Closer examination shows that the red-brick walls have thin white lines running across them, and that the west wall has three much thicker such lines and a deeply recessed entrance with two triangular rooms, one each side, shielding windows from the casual passer-by. There are also concealed windows in the walls. The interior is less spectacular: the walls are all white but the furnishings are black, the altar and font of black porphyry. There are rather crude statues of St Anthony and St Paul by Danny Clahane. Behind the altar in the narrow sanctuary is a sea green Crucifixion window.

References: Pevsner, 4, pp. 551–2; Leonard, pp. 326–8.

St Paul, Tottenham

Status: in use.

Location: Park Lane, between Vicarage Road and Sutherland Road.

Nearest station: White Hart Lane.

Constructed: 1971-7.

Architects: Biscoe & Stanton.

This is a replacement for a Victorian church: the site was redeveloped for housing and the new church was integrated into this. Thus the entrance is beneath flats, whereas from the other side the narrow elevation appears to be squeezed between two large blocks of accommodation, although it does display to the outside world a statue and a bell, which is hung, unusually, in a tall niche in the wall. Inside, the impression of height combined with narrowness is confirmed. The liturgical design remains traditional, with an altar at the east end, on a shallow dais, and behind a brick wall relieved only by a banner of St Paul hung on it. There are a number of statues: the Anglo-Catholic ethos of the previous church has been continued.

Reference: Pevsner, 4, p. 573.

Harrow

St Andrew, Roxbourne

Status: in use.

Location: Malvern Avenue, south side, near junction with Merlin Avenue.

Nearest station: Rayners Lane.

Constructed: 1954–6.

Architect: Michael Farey.

This is one of those underrated churches of the mid 1950s which can now be appreciated more fully. A mission hall was established in 1941 but a permanent church needed the drive of the Revd Edward Nadkarni to make it reality. He raised money locally and funds came also from the bombed church of St Stephen, Poplar. The architect designed a substantial building in a debased Gothic style, with a tall tower over the porch topped by a spire. It is of pale brick, with a polygonal apse and an exposed portal frame of concrete within. Many of the furnishings came from bombed churches: the pews and pulpit were originally in St Mary, Edmonton, and some of the bells in St Thomas, Bethnal Green. However the most striking feature is a set of 49 stained glass windows, all by Dutch artist Max Nauta, in a series of scenes from both Testaments and including a *Christus Rex* in a star shaped window over the altar.

Reference: Pevsner, 3, p. 283.

St Michael & All Angels, Harrow Weald

Status: in use.

Location: Bishop Ken Road, corner College Hill Road.

Nearest station: Harrow & Wealdstone.

Constructed: 1958.

Architect: Thomas F. Ford.

Ford here produced one of his typically well-detailed buildings, which replaced the adjoining hall of 1935. The church is liturgically conventional, low and brick-built, but with a small bell cupola. There is a porch area with a statue of St Michael by D.P. Koningsburger above it. The interior, as often with Ford's designs, has some neo-Georgian touches and pastel colours. Also, again as with many Ford churches, on the shallow apse behind the altar is a large painting by Hans Feibusch depicting St Michael and angels.

Reference: Pevsner, 3, p. 275.

Havering

All Saints, Squirrels Heath

Status: in use.

Location: Ardleigh Green Road, east side, south of junction with Cecil Avenue.

Nearest station: Gidea Park.

Constructed: 1957.

Architect: Rex Foster of Tooley & Foster.

The former church of All Saints in Squirrels Heath Lane was hit by a mine in 1941 and completely destroyed. In 1951 a temporary church was built on the same site, but it was then decided that the parish boundaries should be redrawn and the permanent church should be sited further away from others, in part of what had been the parish of St Andrew, Hornchurch. The new church is a simple brick building, built without any concession to the Liturgical Movement, but functional. It is topped by a small bellcote. The only glass which is not clear is the east window: this has a depiction of wine, wheat and bread in chunk glass designed by John Sutton. The reredos is a gold curtain hung on the east wall, which was originally grey but in 2000 was redecorated in magnolia to match the other walls. The ceiling is blue with white ribs: the feeling given is of spaciousness and the overall design, despite its lack of originality, works well.

Reference: Pevsner, 5, p. 176.

St Augustine, Rush Green

Status: in use.
Location: Birkbeck Road, corner Rush Green Road.
Nearest station: Romford.
Constructed: 1958.
Architect: not known.

This church was constructed in 1958 to replace a hut, which had been used for worship in the area since 1948. It became a parish church in 1969. Unlike many new foundations since the War, it is strongly Anglo-Catholic in its tradition. The building is unpretentious externally, built of brick with a campanile, which proclaims the presence of the church to the passer-by. Originally it was a dual purpose building, but a separate hall was later added. The interior is now painted white, with a rood hung behind the altar.

St George, Harold Hill

Status: in use.

Location: Chippenham Road, opposite junction with Farnham Road.

Nearest station: Harold Wood.

Constructed: 1952-3.

Architect: J.J. Crowe.

This church was designed by the Chelmsford diocesan architect in 1952-3 to serve part of the burgeoning Harold Hill Estate. The original plain brick-built building was substantially rebuilt in 1984-5, and again in 1997, when an entrance with much glass above was added, also in brick but not matching and it is now a church with centre attached. Although it looks down on the shopping centre, no proper use was made of the sloping site and the result is an unhappy mix of styles which impresses not at all. The interior is all painted white with a low ceiling and no furnishings of any note.

Reference: Pevsner, 5, p. 166.

St James, Collier Row
Status: in use.
Location: Chase Cross Road, corner Mount Pleasant Road.
Nearest station: Romford.
Constructed: 1954-6.
Architect: not known.
This is a small unpretentious yellow brick church built along the main road, which doubles as a hall. It looks from the outside much like a Territorial Army centre or the like, but it does have a small and somewhat timid bellcote topped with a cross, and a further external cross on the east wall. The interior is the usual white and the furnishings of little interest.

.

St John & St Matthew, South Hornchurch

Status: in use.
Location: South End Road, corner St Matthew's Close.
Nearest station: Rainham.
Constructed: 1957.
Architects: Ronald Wylde Associates.

A mission hall was erected between the wars from the parish of St Nicholas, Elm Park: after the war the hall was passed to St Helen, Rainham, and the present building was erected next to it. It became a parish church in 1992. The building is of brick, with much higher walls than many similar hall/churches of the era, with long clear windows. The interior is clear and, as with many Evangelical churches in recent times, the regrettable decision has been made to remove the altar from the east wall and to reposition in against one of the longer walls, with chairs around in a semi-circle as if for a public meeting. The interior is white, save for two panels which are a vivid blue, with a blue cross protruding from them.

Reference: Pevsner, 5, p. 176.

St Luke, Cranham Park

Status: in use.
Location: Front Lane, opposite Briarleas Gardens.
Nearest station: Upminster.
Constructed: 2002.
Architect: John Marsh of MEB Partnership.

Cranham is the on the very edge of the built-up area of Greater London, now encircled by the M25. In this bungalow town a yellow brick church with campanile was established in 1957 and ancillary rooms were built in the 1960s. By 2002 the congregation had grown so much that the old church was demolished and replaced, but the new building was attached to the existing two-storey block of rooms. Also in yellow brick, it features a very dated-looking clock turret and small tower, with the portion nearest to the road having further rooms. The interior of the new building has white walls which contrast with the blue/purple carpet and inset area behind the altar, and reddish chairs. The altar is plain, beneath and arch, and is surrounded by guitars, in accordance with modern Evangelical practice, which this interior exemplifies. However, unusual features are a raised glass fronted gallery on three walls, and an immersion font beneath the sanctuary area.

St Nicholas, Elm Park

Status: in use.

Location: St Nicholas Avenue, corner Woodcote Avenue.

Nearest station: Elm Park.

Constructed: 1955-6.

Architect: J.J. Crowe.

This is one of the last works by the Chelmsford diocesan architect and is an astonishingly conservative design for that date, looking back to the designer's work between the wars. It is of red brick, with a somewhat oddly proportioned tower with a louvred top section capped by a green copper roof. There are chapels to north and south, in additions to the main building which are somewhat angular. Inside, the look is again retrospective, with a wood-covered barrel vault above the chancel and arches to the aisles affording glimpses of the side chapels. Above the blue dossal curtain is a striking three light window of Our Lord by Terence Randall, added in 1966.

Reference: Pevsner, 5, p. 176.

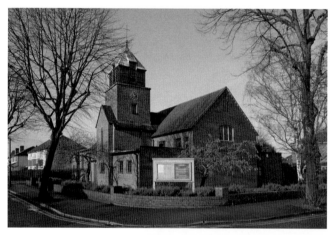

St Paul, Harold Hill

Status: in use.
Location: Petersfield Road, corner Hucknall Close.
Nearest station: Harold Wood.
Constructed: 1953.
Architect: Probably J.J. Crowe.

As with the other church in the very substantial post-war estate of Harold Hill, an opportunity was missed here. The small brick church was screened from the main road by trees and subsequently a large hall has been built in front of it. Unlike the neighbouring Roman Catholic Church of Our Holy Redeemer, St Paul does not proclaim itself to the passer-by. The interior is plain and white and has been remodelled so that the altar and dossal have been moved from the east end to one of the nave walls, with free-standing chairs arranged around it.

Reference: Pevsner, 5, p. 166.

Other Churches

Moor Lane Church, Cranham
A small and somewhat nondescript hall on the corner of Moor Lane and Fairholme Gardens was taken over in 1983 by the ultra-Evangelical St. Luke, Cranham, and has been used since then. There are plans to redevelop by creating a frontage of more ecclesiastical appearance and enlarging the rooms available for facilities, but these have not yet been carried through.

St. Cedd, Romford
This is a small and basic brick-built church hall for the deaf in Sims Close, Romford.

St. Luke, Cranham Park
The yellow brick church with campanile built here in 1957 was replaced in 2002- see the main entry.

St. Matthew, Hornchurch
A small and rather nondescript church/hall in Chelmsford Drive was opened in 1956 and remains in use: its main exterior feature is a large brick cross in the east wall.

Hillingdon

Christ Church, Harlington

Status: in use
Location: Waltham Avenue, at far end.
Nearest station: Hayes & Harlington.
Constructed: 1965.
Architect: not known.
This represents one of the nadirs of 1960s design: a series of small brick boxes
with high windows, save in the slightly elevated section, which has longer
openings.

St Edmund the King, Northwood Hills

Status: in use.

Location: Pinner Road, near the junction with Alandale Drive.

Nearest station: Northwood Hills.

Constructed: 1964.

Architect: N.F. Cachemaille-Day.

Cachemaille-Day is often thought of as an inter-war architect, but he did not die until 1976 and designed a number of churches after 1945. This was one of his last and also one of the more conventional: a tall brick building with typical elongated windows above the entrance. It replaced a hall, which had been used as the church since 1935 and the chancel of that building was incorporated as the lady chapel of this. The additional feature of the church is that all the stained glass is the work of Michael Farrer-Bell and was installed over a period of 22 years. As with most of Cachemaille-Day's churches, the tradition is of moderate Anglo-Catholicism.

St Edmund of Canterbury, Yeading

Status: in use.

Location: Edmunds Close, off Yeading Lane.

Nearest station: Hayes & Harlington.

Constructed: 1961.

Architect: Anthony Lewis.

This is one of two churches in the locality, both designed by the same architect. It replaced a timber hall. The building is of yellow brick and is of traditional design, with chancel, nave, and a lady chapel: the chancel is raised by three steps from the nave in a very conservative design for the time. There is a west bell tower, almost but not quite detached.

Reference: Pevsner, 3, p. 369.

St George, Heathrow

Status: in use.
Location: Opposite the car park for Terminal 2.
Nearest station: Heathrow Terminals 1-3.
Constructed: 1968.
Architect: Jack Forrest.

This was designed as an ecumenical chapel for travellers and visitors: initially there were three apses, one for Anglicans, one for Roman Catholics, and one for Nonconformists: however, there is now only one altar. The building is approached through an enclosed courtyard with a large cross and is designed as a vaulted crypt, taking inspiration from Early Christian precedents.

References: Pevsner, 3, p. 332.

St Mary, South Ruislip

Status: in use.

Location: The Fairway, east side, near junction with Long Lane.

Nearest station: South Ruislip.

Constructed: 1959.

Architect: Laurence King.

This is one of the rare outposts of Forward in Faith in the suburbs and in post-1945 churches. Above the entrance on the west wall is a large crucifix by Brian Asquith: around it is a concrete frame, with pale yellow bricks. There is a clerestory giving light to the interior, and behind the high altar is a polygonal east end with small coloured windows by Keith New. The vicarage and hall adjoin and the whole is a composite design.

References: Pevsner, 3, p. 347.

St Nicholas, Hayes

Status: in use.

Location: Raynton Drive, corner Lansbury Drive.

Nearest station: Northolt.

Constructed: 1961.

Architect: Anthony Lewis.

This church has some similarities to the nearby St Edmund, also designed by Lewis. It also has a tall bell tower which is almost detached from the main building of the church, and the wall to the street is almost completely brick with high slit windows.

Reference: Pevsner, 3, p. 369.

Hounslow

All Saints, Hanworth

Status: in use.

Location: Uxbridge Road, corner Woodlawn Drive.

Nearest station: Feltham.

Constructed: 1952.

Architect: N.F. Cachemaille-Day.

This is a very unusual, albeit striking, design by Cachemaille-Day, which was built in two separate phases. It was originally intended to build only a Nissen hut, but the architect himself suggested an incremental approach, which was made possible by money from the damaged St Mary, Haggerston. The first stage provided a long low building in yellow brick with what is now a lady chapel and baptistery. The second phase, finished in 1957, is now the main church, and was constructed to accord with what was already there. It is a cube with a lantern above, and with rooms off on each side save for the east end, which has an apse to hold an altar on four concrete columns. Concrete was also used for the font, which was decorated by the architect with the seven sacraments. There is stained glass in the lady chapel by Goddard & Gibbs. This is one of the best churches in London of its age.

References: Pevsner, 3, pp. 420-1; Leonard, pp. 313-14.

All Saints, Isleworth

Status: in use.

Location: Church Street, north side, near junction with Park Road.

Nearest station: Isleworth.

Reconstructed: 1967-70.

Architect: Michael Blee.

Both All Saints, Isleworth and Holy Trinity, Hounslow, were largely destroyed by fire in 1943. In both cases rebuilding did not take place for a very long time. Blee was not appointed as architect until 1963 and work did not start until 1967. To the original fifteenth-century tower and nave of 1706 he added a modern red brick building, which is a definite statement of modernity, displaying concrete fin like structures at the corners and with very angle of the building of 90 degrees. The entrance is surmounted by a wall of glass and the interior with its brick walls is a clear contrast to what went before. There is a gallery in the west end and stained glass by Keith New, as well as some monuments from the old church.

References: Pevsner, 3, pp. 429-30; Leonard, pp. 320-2.

Good Shepherd, West Hounslow

Status: in use.

Location: Beavers Lane, corner Great South West Road.

Nearest station: Hounslow West

Constructed: 1956.

Architect: Michael Farey.

This church was constructed as a result of compensation being made available from the destroyed St John, Wapping. It was built as a hall/church but with two separate areas at right-angles, which can be combined if required. The building is of the typical red brick boxy style of the time, with a small but prominent bell tower. There are a set of seven stained glass windows by Luxford Studios, which depict the destruction of St John and the new church here as well as saints. The church has developed an Anglo-Catholic ethos and there are a number of statues.

Holy Angels, Cranford

Status: in use.

Location: High Street, opposite The Avenue.

Nearest station: Hatton Cross.

Constructed: 1970.

Architect: Norman Haines Design Partnership.

This replaced two successive temporary churches, both on the Bath Road: the opportunity was taken to move the new church to the centre of the village. The building is a barn, of brick with high windows illuminating the interior. A large Christus Rex is hung on the east wall over the altar. There is a separate lady chapel separated by glass from the nave. Since the incumbency of the Revd Maurice Child, the parish has been strongly Anglo-Catholic and this is reflected in the furnishings. It is a striking contrast to the old parish church of St Dunstan.

Reference: Pevsner, 3, p. 412.

Holy Trinity, Hounslow
Status: in use.
Location: High Street, opposite School Road.
Nearest station: Hounslow East.
Constructed: 1961.
Architect: W.E. Cross.
As with the nearby All Saints, Isleworth, this church was destroyed by fire in 1943 and has been rebuilt in contemporary style: unlike Isleworth, however, there was no part of the old building left, save for some monuments which are housed in the crypt. The design is very much of its time, with very tall concrete tower with a fibreglass sculpture of the Holy Trinity by Wilfred Dudeny. The entrance leads through a coffee shop into a lengthy nave with slit pale blue windows and concrete ribs. The lady chapel and crypt are beneath. The altar is a large white stone, again typical of its period.

Reference: Pevsner, 3, p. 425.

St Mary, Isleworth

Status: in use.

Location: Worton Road, corner Bridge Road.

Nearest station: Isleworth.

Constructed: 1954.

Architect: H.S. Goodhart-Rendel.

This was an early post-war construction and was built to replace a hall, which is still in use for secular purposes. As with most of this architect's designs, it is of Gothic inspiration but with idiosyncratic interpretations. It is low and of brick, with steeply graded roofs and prominent transepts. Inside, the arches which intersect at the crossing, are, perhaps surprisingly, round-headed: the interior is pale grey. The reredos is, unusually, of painted tiles and depicts the Virgin and Child with scenes from the Bible around. There is a separate lady chapel and some stained glass. Regrettably the interior has now been altered and turned round.

References: Pevsner, 3, p. 430; SPWC, p. 32.

St Paul, Brentford

Status: in use.

Location: St Paul's Road, north side.

Nearest station: Brentford.

Reconstructed: 1990.

Architect: Michael Blee.

The church, by Francis & Francis, 1868-9, had become in need of substantial renovation by 1990. The fine tower with spire were left, and the new design incorporated the chancel walls and the south walls of the nave. The former nave was adapted as a vestibule and café, and the former chancel as a chapel. The new church, hexagonal in form but with three triangular oratories running off it, has a central altar and finely designed woodwork in the swooping ceilings.

References: Pevsner, 3, pp. 378-9; Leonard, pp. 322-4.

St Richard of Chichester, Hanworth

Status: in use.

Location: Forge Lane, far end.

Nearest station: Hampton.

Constructed: 1964.

Architect: Leslie Channing.

Just inside the borough is this small building, which can be seen from afar because above the large gables in the roof are four concrete columns meeting high above, surmounted by a cross.

Reference: Pevsner, 3, p. 421.

Islington

Emmanuel, Upper Holloway

Status: in use.

Location: Hornsey Road, west side, south of junction with Seven Sisters Road.

Nearest station: Finsbury Park.

Constructed: 1988.

Architect: Keith Harrison.

The south aisle only of a Victorian church of 1884 remains and has been incorporated into a new church. The architect used very considerable ingenuity: the roof slopes south to north from the former wall and an entrance porch with triangular roof stands out in front.

Reference: Pevsner, 4, p. 654.

St George and All Saints, Tufnell Park

Status: in use.
Location: Crayford Road, corner Caerleon Road.
Nearest station: Caledonian Road.
Constructed: 1972-5.
Architect: Clive Alexander.
The former St George in Tufnell Park Road was converted to a theatre and this was built as its replacement. It is a red brick cube with a flat roof which projects on three sides. The interior resembles at first glance a sports hall, with lighting from above and also through some slit windows, and a flat ceiling on thin blue piers. There is an external detached bell tower and near to that a large wooden cross.

Reference: Pevsner, 4, p. 655.

St Stephen, Canonbury

Status: in use.

Location: Canonbury Road, north side, east of Canonbury Grove.

Nearest station: Essex Road.

Reconstructed: 1958.

Architect: A. Llewellyn-Smith.

This church was built in 1837-9 by Inwood and Clifton but later extended. It was reconstructed after war damage in 1957-8 so that the interior was completely transformed. In particular, the interior was turned completely around east to west, and a wall painting of the martyrdom of the patron saint by Brian Thomas was added. The only remaining furnishing from the former church is the nineteenth-century reredos. There is a window by Carl Edwards. The tone is traditional Islington Evangelicalism.

Reference: Pevsner, 4, p. 659.

Other Churches

All Saints, Islington
The former church, known as All Saints, Battle Bridge, was closed and in 1977 replaced by a simple church/hall on the corner of Caledonian Road and Carnegie Street.

Church on the Corner, Islington
In 1994 a group from All Saints, Islington, took over a former pub at 64 Barnsbury Road, and converted it to a 'new kind of church'. Externally it still resembles what it was before.

St Anne, Poole's Park
A Victorian church in Durham Road was replaced in 1960 by a building by R.B. Craze, which had a very short life and was in turn demolished in the 1970s.

St Francis of Assisi, West Holloway
A small pale brick church of no architectural interest was constructed in 1976 in North Road, but soon became surplus to requirements and is now let for secular purposes.

St Luke, Finsbury
In 1977 Biscoe & Stanton designed this architecturally uninteresting small church centre, but it has never been consecrated and is not set out as a church.

St Peter, Upper Holloway
The fine church by C.L. Luck, 1879, has been converted to flats. It was replaced in 1979 by a small modern building adjacent to it, which is not now used for services.

Kensington & Chelsea

St Helen, North Kensington

Status: in use.

Location: St Quintin Avenue, corner St Helen's Gardens.

Nearest station: Ladbroke Grove.

Constructed: 1954-6.

Architect: J.B.S. Comper.

Sebastian Comper was a competent but rarely inspired architect whose reputation is rightly overshadowed by his father. Here he built a replacement for a church destroyed in the War, in pale brick and in a very late Gothic style. The traditional feel is accentuated by the insertion of a lectern from the former church, pews from Holy Trinity, Latimer Road, and an organ case and some windows by Sir Ninian Comper. The interior is whitewashed and somewhat anaemic. The tone is now much more Evangelical than it was when the church was erected.

References: Pevsner, 3, p. 457; Clarke, p. 111.

St John with St Andrew, Chelsea

Status: in use.

Location: World's End Estate, King's Road.

Nearest station: Fulham Broadway.

Constructed: 2000.

Architects: H.T. Cadbury Brown & Partners.

This replaced an Edwardian church by Blomfield, and is a raised red brick polygon, with a projection from it, somewhat overshadowed by towering blocks of flats around. The interior is modern Evangelical and thus bare, with not even a font, and the altar has been pushed behind the drum kit.

St Thomas, Kensal Town

Status: in use.

Location: Kensal Road, corner East Row.

Nearest station: Westbourne Park.

Constructed: 1967.

Architect: R.B. Craze.

Romilly Craze is another architect whose work is underrated, although here he attempted to modernise his style, with not particularly successful results. This is a brick rectangle with all the windows elevated. It was constructed to replace a church destroyed in the War – in other words about 25 years previously. There is a fibreglass statue of the patron saint, by A.W. Banks, on the otherwise blank exterior west wall, and the interior has many shrines and the like, which brighten the unrelieved white walls.

Reference: Pevsner, 3, p. 462.

Kingston on Thames

St Mark, Surbiton

Status: in use.

Location: St Mark's Hill, corner Church Hill Road.

Nearest station: Surbiton.

Constructed: 1960.

Architect: R.B. Craze.

St Mark was another Victorian church (1845) which was badly damaged by
bombing. An air raid in 1940 destroyed all but the tower and spire. It was
reconstructed in 1960 by Craze, to re-create what had been there before but
with improvements. The editors of Pevsner say that it was 'rebuilt in a deplorable
style': the historian of the parish on the other hand says of Craze that he was 'a
man of vision and of devotion … every suggestion of the church was carefully
received, interpreted or rejected, to impose a unity on the whole restoration'.
It was anachronistic by 1960 to rebuild on the original plan, although some
deficiencies in the former church were provided, such as providing a lady chapel.
The only modern note was provided by the sanctuary and altar being moved
forward from the east end nearer to the congregation. The choir and organ were
originally moved to a west gallery but later returned to a more conventional
place in the south aisle. In 2011 reordering began together with the provision of
a new hall on the north side. The church was provided with new stained glass: the
west window and the St George window are by W. Carter Shapland, and the east
and lady chapel windows by J. Dowling. The woodwork was traditionally carved
and there is a Majestas by Anthony Southwell. This rebuilding was the height of
conservative liturgical thinking in the period.

Reference: Pevsner, 2, pp. 322-3.

Lambeth

All Saints, Clapham Park

Status: in use.

Location: Lyham Road, corner Saxby Road.

Nearest station: Streatham Hill.

Constructed: 1982.

Architects: Richard Watson & Partners.

This church is a replacement for a Victorian building (1858 by Talbot Bury & Hering). As with other churches, the replacement was intended to be cheaper to heat and run and to provide additional accommodation. To that end, the architect designed three spaces, one for worship, one for a hall and one as an assembly area, which can be joined by folding back flexible screens. The building itself is on an elongated cruciform plan, of yellow brick with pitched roofs and with a lantern at the central crossing. The tradition of the church is Evangelical and there are few internal furnishings, although there is a somewhat crude baldachino over the altar, but it was well provided with stained glass and even has a rose window.

All Saints, West Dulwich

Status: in use.
Location: Rosendale Road, corner Lovelace Road.
Nearest station: West Dulwich.
Reconstructed: 2006.
Architects: Thomas F. Ford & Partners.

All Saints has had many vicissitudes. The original church was a marvellous late Victorian design by G.H. Fellowes Prynne (1887-91), which was never finished. It was badly damaged in the war and restored by J.B.S. Comper. In 2000 it was burned out, leaving only the massive walls. It was decided to rebuild: the site of the building is incomparable, because of the way in which it dominates the steep slope. The architects reused the walls and reconstructed the roofs using modern designs, and finally completed the west end left unfinished by Fellowes Prynne. The new western extension is constructed of matching red brick, but in an uncompromisingly modern style which does not aim to imitate what was left. It features areas of white stone, including a semi-circular arched entrance which wraps around the outside. Inside the former building, the stained glass has been replaced by clear, so that the building is now flooded with light. New small chairs have been provided which can be moved as required and the sanctuary arrangements have been simplified, with a small altar brought forward. The architects have managed to adapt to the challenges provided by the immense size of the interior. The tradition has always been Liberal Catholic, but there are now few furnishings.

Christ Church, Gipsy Hill

Status: in use.
Location: Gipsy Hill, corner Highland Road.
Nearest station: Gipsy Hill.
Constructed: 1987.
Architect: Brian Drury.

This is another church where a fire destroyed the former Victorian church (1867 by John Giles), leaving only the very substantial tower, which had been added later. The opportunity was taken to construct an entirely new hexagonal-shaped church which was linked both to the tower and to the church hall. The new church, of pale brick, has large clear windows on either side of the altar and a conical roof supported by visible trusses. The external appearance is somewhat fragmented, as the sides of the chancel and the wall behind the altar and between the windows project upwards , for no apparent reason. The tradition is one of what is termed 'Open Evangelicalism' and thus the furnishings are few in number but of pleasant light wood. There are substantial rails on three sides of the small altar.

Emmanuel, West Dulwich

Status: in use.

Location: Clive Road, east side, north of junction with Chalford Road.

Nearest station: Gipsy Hill.

Constructed: 1967.

Architects: Hutchison Locke & Monte.

This replaced a Victorian building of 1876 by E.C. Robins which was destroyed by fire. The new church incorporated a youth club and some housing was also constructed on the site. It is small, box-like, and with few windows, much of the light coming from roof lights above the altar. Some of the brick walls inside have received whitewash, others are left as they are, including the far wall of the sanctuary. The chairs are arranged on three sides of the altar. There is a bell tower which is equally angular, and a bridge office under which is the entrance.

Reference: Pevsner, 2, p. 333.

Immanuel & St Andrew, Streatham

Status: in use.
Location: Streatham High Road, west side, near ice rink.
Nearest station: Streatham.
Constructed: 1989.
Architect: Nigel Melhuish.

Immanuel Church was constructed in 1854 and reconstructed by Benjamin
Ferrey in 1864 so that it could hold a congregation of 1,000. It had a substantial
tower providing a presence on the main road. By the 1970s the cost of
maintaining the structure was becoming oppressive and then the heating system
failed. The church was demolished, apart from the tower, and the contents,
including the stained glass sold: continuity was not promoted save that a chapel
was constructed in the foot of the tower. Part of the site went for housing. The
new building is hidden from the road and adjoins the earlier parish hall, from
which it is divided by a folding partition. The main worship area uses the same
space as the former nave and chancel, but is low, with a swooping wooden
roof, and the sanctuary is placed on the long external wall in accordance with
prevailing trends. The congregation are thus very near to the altar, a complete
reversal from Victorian thought.

St Agnes, Kennington Park

Status: in use.

Location: St Agnes Place, east side.

Nearest station: Oval.

Constructed: 1956.

Architect: Ralph Covell.

This church has received more criticism than most: the editors of Pevsner describe it as 'a building of no importance'. The brickbats arise from the failure of the Diocese to rebuild its noble predecessor, which was damaged by bombing, but those throwing them do not consider how such a building would have been funded and filled. In fact the new church is compact, well designed, easy to heat and has a substantial atmosphere within because it uses the reredos from the old church, by Temple Moore, and a number of candlesticks and the like. Some items have returned from Holy Spirit, Southsea, where they had been accommodated because Stephen Dykes-Bower was concerned both with rebuilding the old church here and with repairing the church in Portsmouth. There are ancillary rooms attached, and the traditional plan includes a lady chapel and aisles on each side. The church is of pale brick with a pitched roof and a small flèche. The tradition of Anglo-Catholicism has been continued and the interior is extremely well cared for.

References: Pevsner, 2, p. 334; Clarke, p. 253.

189

St James, Clapham Park

Status: in use.

Location: between Park Hill and Briarwood Road.

Nearest station: Clapham Common.

Constructed: 1957-8.

Architect: N.F. Cachemaille-Day.

The former church, originally constructed in 1829 by Vulliamy, was destroyed in 1940. Its replacement is one of the most interesting post-war designs, combining a traditional layout with some modern ideas: it has similarities with some of Cachemaille-Day's more radical interwar designs. The building is of yellowish brick with a campanile on the south side near the west end. Internally, an impression of Gothic influence comes from the concrete ribs, which meet where the aisle less nave moves into the aisled chancel. Above the west door is a characteristic five-light window, but the most striking feature is a low, deeply coloured, east window, which forms an unusual but highly effective reredos. The architect designed the windows, which were made by A.F. Erridge.

References: Pevsner, 2, pp. 380-1; Clarke, pp. 217-18; Leonard, pp. 312-13.

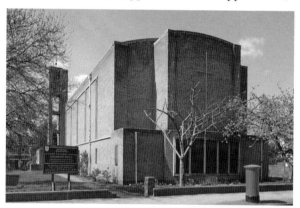

St Stephen, Clapham Park
Status: in use.
Location: Weir Road opposite Radbourne Road.
Nearest station: Clapham South.
Constructed: 1974.
Architect: not known.
This replaced a Victorian church (1867 by Knowles) which was demolished when
the area around was redeveloped. It was replaced by this much smaller building,
a single storey worship area with ancillary rooms attached of little architectural
excitement: it resembles a nursery school. Internally, the walls are brick and the
ceiling low.

St Stephen, South Lambeth.

Status: in use.

Location: St Stephen's Terrace corner Wilkinson Street.

Nearest station: Stockwell.

Constructed: 1969.

Architect: Norman Ashley Green.

The present building replaced a vast Victorian church of 1860-1 by J. Barnett, which required an Act of Parliament to be demolished. The new, much smaller, church reflected its time but proved impracticable, albeit for different reasons. The architect designed it in the shape of a pentangle, with a roof soaring up but so that it was dark within and without. It was lit only by slit windows. It was usable only by the fit. The entrance was invisible to all but those in the know. In 2006 it was extensively renovated by inserting large windows, a totally new glass entrance with facilities for the disabled, and a suspended ceiling which reflected light. A new parish room, also mainly of glass, was constructed next to the entrance. The striking characteristics of the church have been retained but it has been made easy and welcoming for the congregation.

Other Churches

St Paul with St Saviour, Brixton

In 1981 St Paul was made redundant and the congregation moved to a small, angular, brick building designed by John Soper in 1958 for the Seventh Day Adventists. It is in Ferndale Road.

St Mary, Lambeth

On the redundancy of the historic church of St Mary at Lambeth in 1972, the congregation moved to the Lambeth Methodist Mission in Lambeth Road, which is now a united Anglican/Methodist church. It replaces a bombed church and is not dissimilar to many Anglican buildings of the 1950s – brick-built and plain.

Lewisham

Good Shepherd, Lee

Status: in use.

Location: Handen Road, corner Wantage Road.

Nearest station: Lee.

Constructed: 1956-7.

Architect: T.F. Ford.

This was another competent post-war production by Thomas F. Ford. The former church, by Ernest Newton (1881) was largely destroyed in 1941 and a temporary post-war chapel was erected. In 1957 the new building was erected, using the former foundations, and in some places considerable parts of the old walls. The basic plan is a simple rectangle, but from the outside it is clear that the internal pattern is cruciform: there are transepts north and south, and also aisles with characteristic arches. The windows are round-headed and each transept has also a circular glass. There is a very small copper flèche above the crossing. The chancel and nave have barrel-roofed ceilings. Many of the fittings, including some fine choir stalls by George Gilbert Scott, came from the demolished church of St Peter, Lee, in the adjoining Borough of Greenwich. In 1990 the west end was divided off to form a hall.

Reference: Clarke, p. 242.

St George, Perry Hill

Status: in use.
Location: Vancouver Road, corner Woolstone Road.
Nearest station: Catford.
Constructed: 2004-5.
Architects: Thomas F. Ford & Partners.

St George, Perry Hill, was a very large Victorian church of no particular architectural merit, designed by W.C. Banks in 1878-80. It suffered a serious fire in 1976 but some time after repairs were carried out subsidence made it unsafe to use and the congregation moved into the church hall. In 1999 it was demolished and a new, smaller church constructed with housing on the rest of the site. So much is a familiar story, but the difference here is that instead of a featureless slab, as in so many cases, Thomas F. Ford & Partners, based in nearby Sydenham, produced a modernised version of a Gothic church, in bright red brick, incorporating the fine rose window from the old church, with glass by Henry Holiday. The new church has pitched roofs: the north roof is much longer as it covers ancillary accommodation on that side and through it rises a clock tower with spire above in grand style. The rose window, which depicts Christ in the centre light with angels around, has beneath it nine other windows brought from the former building. All the interior furnishings are of matching pale wood, which creates a sense of unity and also a contrast with the brightly coloured Victorian glass. The walls are white. This is a remarkable building for its date.

St James, Hatcham

Status: in use.

Location: St James's, far end.

Nearest station: New Cross Gate.

Constructed: 1982.

Architect: Raymond Hall.

In 1980 the Victorian church (by W.B.L. Granville, 1849-54) was closed and handed over to the adjoining Goldsmiths' College. The church, once notorious for the ministry of the 'Ritualist martyr', Father Arthur Tooth, is now neglected and empty. The congregation moved next door to what had been the ground floor of a youth club, which was converted for the purpose and has very recently been refurbished. The pulpit, lectern, font, altar frontal, and some stained glass were integrated into the new building: the church is a rectangular auditorium-like area with a simple sanctuary in an alcove. Whether Tooth would have approved is debatable, but certainly it is easy to maintain.

St Laurence, Catford

Status: in use.
Location: Bromley Road, east side, between Culverley and Penerley Roads.
Nearest station: Catford Bridge.
Constructed: 1967–8.
Architect: Ralph Covell.

The former St Laurence, by H.R. Gough, 1886–7, was demolished in order to build a car park which was never in fact constructed. The new building was thus on a virgin site. Covell's design was thought at the time to be revolutionary but has dated quickly. It is octagonal and the Lady Chapel off the main building is pentagonal. The building is of brick, but the main external feature is a concrete frame, which is exposed and is surmounted in the case of the octagon by a corona and in the case of the pentagon by an open framed spire with one bell. The interior is contemporary and has perhaps worn a little better: the space is used so that the altar is in a circular area with the seats facing from in front and on two sides: behind is an illuminated circle with a large cross of multicoloured glass hung in front of it. The lady chapel is in more restful colours but the layout is similar. A war memorial window from the old church has been reinstalled.

References: Pevsner, 2, p. 414; Leonard, pp. 319-20.

St Mark, Downham

Status: in use.

Location: Castillon Road, corner Baudwin Road.

Nearest station: Bellingham.

Constructed: about 1960.

Architect: not known.

A pre-fab church was established after the War, appropriately enough to serve a pre-fab estate. It was replaced about 1960 by this simple low brick, barrel-roofed building which is far more impressive within than without. In common with other churches in the neighbourhood, it reflects a moderate Anglo-Catholicism and there is a dignified altar with six candlesticks and a traditional crucifix on the white wall behind: the building has been provided with other homely statues.

St Michael, Lower Sydenham

Status: in use.
Location: Champion Crescent, within the crescent.
Nearest station: Lower Sydenham.
Constructed: 1955-6.
Architects: W.H. Hobday & F.J. Maynard.
This was a replacement for a church destroyed by bombing. Its conservative design demonstrates clearly that by the mid 1950s the liturgical movement had made very little progress in middle of the road Anglican thought, with the sanctuary, and then the altar itself, being raised slightly in traditional style. It is tall, brick-built, with a pitched roof constructed on concrete frames which are visible internally, and an abundance of clear glass on each wall, with a small separate north chapel. The height of the nave and chancel results in there being a very tall red dossal at the east end facing an elevated organ in a gallery at the west. There is a miniature tower.

Reference: Clarke, pp. 249-50.

St Philip the Apostle, Sydenham

Status: in use.
Location: Wells Park Road, corner Coombe Lane.
Nearest station: Sydenham.
Constructed: 1984.
Architect: Nigel Melhuish.

This was yet another modern replacement for a demolished Victorian church (1864-7 by Nash and Round). Unremarkable externally, it has pale bricks and wildly asymmetrical pitched roofs, so that even the sanctuary beneath does not have a unified feel to it. There is a church and a hall, which can be combined and either can use the intermediate area between the two. The sanctuary is surprisingly striking, with a Christus Rex figure on the white brick wall behind the altar, which is on a raised concrete platform. There is an alcove in the wall with a tabernacle which has a finely worked door, a number of modern statues and a fine series of stations, showing its moderate Anglo-Catholic teaching.

Other Churches

St Michael, Hatcham
In 1957 a church built over ancillary rooms was constructed to designs by Covell Matthews (shown in *Sixty Post-war Churches,* pp. 94–5) on the foundations of a bombed building. As early as 1971 it was demolished and a community centre was constructed some distance away in Desmond Street, by Gordon Cook. The new church is a small rectangle with seating for 150 and simple wooden furnishings: the complex has no architectural merit or interest.

Merton

Ascension, Pollards Hill

Status: in use.

Location: Greenwood Road, corner Sherwood Park Road.

Nearest station: Norbury.

Constructed: 1951-3.

Architects: Caroe & Partners.

The first post-war church to be dedicated in the Diocese of Southwark was The Ascension, which replaced a parish hall built in 1936. It is built of red brick, of simple design with pitched roof, and having remarkably narrow aisles on each side divided from the nave by hardwood covered columns. It has an apsidal baptistery at the west end and although there is no chancel arch, there is a brick arch over the altar step. The church has a tradition of Southwark Liberal Anglo-Catholicism.

Reference: SPWC, p. 19.

Emmanuel, Morden

Status: in use.
Location: Dudley Drive, near junction with Kingsbridge Road.
Nearest station: Morden South or St Helier.
Constructed: 1962.
Architect: K.C. White.
This is a small yellow brick building within the Evangelical tradition of Morden. It is rectangular, with a shallow pitched roof and metal framed windows. The most notable feature is a small matching bell-tower with louvred timber belfry, without bells.

Reference: Pevsner, 2, p. 447.

Holy Cross, Motspur Park

Status: in use.

Location: Adela Avenue, corner Douglas Avenue.

Nearest station: Motspur Park.

Constructed: 1949.

Architect: Ralph Covell.

This was the first new church constructed in London after the Second World War, during a period of acute shortages. An earlier building constructed in 1914 had been demolished by a flying bomb. The designer of the replacement was Ralph Covell, who produced a building appropriate to the straitened times. It looks externally rather like a somewhat domestic church hall, and is of rendered concrete blocks, with pitched roof, many internal exposed beams and traditional pews. There is a carved rood group on the beam above the altar made by students at Kingston School of Art. It has a homely feel which is not always found in more elaborate buildings.

Reference: K. Richardson, *The 'Twenty-Five' Churches of the Southwark Diocese*, London, 2002, pp. 99-100.

208

St James, Merton
Status: in use.
Location: Beaford Grove, corner Martin Way.
Nearest station: South Merton.
Constructed: 1956-7.
Architect: T.F. Ford.
This is an interesting building. It was designed by Ford to replace the former
church, which stands next to it and was then used as a hall. For its date it is
of conservative design and could easily be mistaken for a church of 30 years
previously. It is tall and brick-built with a pitched roof and a tower with a thin
octagonal concrete spire rising above it. There is a concrete figure of St James
above the entrance. As with many of Ford's churches, there is a mural by Hans
Feibusch, in this case a triptych above the altar. The windows have curved heads
and there are two by John Hayward. The furnishings are largely contemporary
and extremely well maintained.

Reference: Pevsner, 2, p. 437.

St Mark, Wimbledon

Status: in use.

Location: St Mark's Place.

Nearest station: Wimbledon.

Constructed: 1968-9.

Architects: Humphreys & Hurst and D.E. Nye & Partners.

Very near the station in Wimbledon is the church of St Mark, which has an unusual and original design in the form of a pentangle with a lantern in the pitched roof above to provide light. The nave has a framed structure of concrete rather akin to a tent. There are aisles with flat roofs, and since the original construction similar extensions have been built to the north west and south east. There is a plain altar in front of the east wall: the opportunity to place it centrally was not taken. The church replaces a Victorian building which burned down.

Reference: Pevsner, 2, p. 452.

St Martin, Morden

Status: in use.

Location: Camborne Road, south side, near junction with Queen Mary Avenue.

Nearest station: Motspur Park.

Constructed: 1957.

Architect: F. Sutton-Smith.

St Martin was constructed simply in order to provide worship in the Evangelical tradition which prevails in Morden. It is built of red and brown brick, with painted metal windows, typically for its date. The main body of the church is a tall barn shape with pitched roof of concrete pantiles, made light by the substantially sized windows. Ancillary rooms adjoin.

St Matthew, Wimbledon

Status: in use.

Location: Durham Road, corner Spenser Road.

Nearest station: Raynes Park.

Constructed: 1958.

Architect: J.B.S. Comper.

St Matthew was built in 1909 as one of the six London churches designed by
Ernest Shearman. It was very badly damaged in the War and was reconstructed
on the same site by Sebastian Comper. Shearman's church was conservative for
its time, although idiosyncratic, and Comper's replacement is equally conservative
without the idiosyncrasy. The church has aisles on each side, an apse containing
the sanctuary, with baldachino over the altar, and a small bellcote. The nave roof
has concrete trusses which are designed to simulate timber. The church could
have been designed at any time in the preceding 30 or 40 years: however, it
does manifest itself to the outside world as an ecclesiastical building, and it has a
pleasing unity. While the baldachino is reminiscent of the architect's distinguished
father, the rose window in the west wall is a tribute to Shearman. A wooden
reredos and a Nativity scene from the former church were saved and have been
reused. The tradition is one of Liberal Anglo-Catholicism.

References: Pevsner, 2, p. 452; J. Salmon, *Ernest Charles Shearman*, pp. 43-60.

Newham

All Saints, West Ham

Status: in use.

Location: East Road, west side, near junction with Portway.

Nearest station: Plaistow.

Constructed: 1969.

Architect: not known.

All Saints, which is a church for the deaf, is confusingly in the parish of the same name. Between the wars a few outstanding churches were built for the deaf community, such as St Saviour, Acton, and St Bede, Clapham. However, in more recent years provision has been more modest and this is an example. It was built in 1969 on the site of a former Congregational church and is a small low brick building with concrete external decoration.

Ascension, Victoria Docks

Status: in use.

Location: Prince of Wales Road, corner Baxter Road.

Nearest station: Prince Regent.

Reconstructed: 1995-6.

Architects: Richard Lyon & Associates.

This church has been internally very substantially reordered while remaining externally much as it was when built as the Felsted School mission by J.E.K. and J.P. Cutts in 1903-7. In 1995-6 the architects effectively cut the building in half through a new entrance which leads to a small café area. To the west are halls which can be used for a variety of activities and to the east is the worship area, which is much reduced in size and has had the chancel lowered. Some of the furnishings have been retained including the fine windows by a variety of artists: one of the nave windows is now visible only from the gentleman's lavatory.

Reference: Pevsner, 5, p. 258.

St Bartholomew, East Ham.

Status: in use.

Location: Barking Road, south side, opposite Ron Leighton Way.

Nearest station: East Ham.

Constructed: 1983.

Architect: APEC.

In Newham there have been a number of conversions and new buildings where the old church had become too large. St Bartholomew was constructed in 1901-4 to meet the pressing need for accommodation. By 1975 it was decided it was redundant and demolished. The new building which replaced it was designed to cater not only for worship, but also for day care, a health centre and housing. The new complex, in dark red brick, is of imposing height because it has three storeys of flats above the church/care/health area. It is set back somewhat but proclaims its presence with a sculpture of the Holy Family by John Bridgeman: he also produced a Crucifixion in the side chapel. The church area is quite small, but can be opened up into the hall behind. The walls are unrelieved white, and the fittings of light wood. The roof slopes down to the altar: only a font remains from the magnificent but rapidly outdated old church.

References: Pevsner, 5, pp. 267-8.

St John, North Woolwich.

Status: in use.

Location: Between Albert Road and Marwood Street.

Nearest station: North Woolwich.

Constructed: 1968.

Architects: Laurence King & Partners.

In the somewhat isolated settlement of North Woolwich, an unusual solution to the problem of declining congregations was reached. The Anglican parish of St John and the Roman Catholic parish of St Mary with St Edward share the building, as does the Jesus People's Church. The building is angular and of very dark brick, with most of the windows elevated. Inside however, it is light and spacious and the nave altar, of green stone, is somewhat isolated. It stands beneath a striking metal corona. There are statues of Our Lady and St Edward in traditional form, from the former Roman church, but modern stations of the cross and abstract slit-shaped stained glass windows. The architects donated the font, which is an African copper cooking pot in a wooden frame.

References: Pevsner, 5, p. 314.

St Luke, Canning Town.

Status: in use.

Location: Ruscoe Road

Nearest station: Canning Town.

Constructed: 2000.

Architects: Ronald Wylde Partnership.

The Victorian church here was deconsecrated in 1985 and converted for medical and other community uses. Its replacement was constructed in 2000: the main church area is used during the week as the hall and gym for the primary school. On Sundays it is opened out into the side chapel and used for services. It is a small octagonal building but prominent because of its stainless steel spire topped with a cross lit by fibre optics. The interior is a curious mixture of old and new: in the brick walls of the chapel and the white walls of the hall are inserted six Kempe windows from the redundant Royal Marines' Chapel at Deal. The chapel also has a mosaic from the old church.

References: Pevsner, 5, p. 259.

St Mark, Beckton.
Status: in use.
Location: Tollgate Road, corner Kingsford Way.
Nearest station: Beckton.
Constructed: 1989.
Architect: APEC.
In the redevelopment of Beckton, APEC were called upon to produce an entirely new church instead of replacing or adapting and existing building. It is usually open, as it is part of a complex, and very well maintained. The interior is far more attractive than would be expected from looking at the exterior, which has roofs running in different direction at different levels and a somewhat confused appearance. Inside, the brick and timbering work well and a small niche was built into one wall to hold a statue of Our Lady. There is high-level lighting around the sanctuary and a small Blessed Sacrament chapel.

References: Pevsner, 5, p. 305.

St Martin, Plaistow
Status: in use.
Location: Boundary Road, corner Claughton Road.
Nearest station: Upton Park.
Reconstructed: 1991-7.
Architects: Cottrell & Vermeulen.
The mission church of 1894 was adapted and converted so that the interior does
not match the exterior, which is of no great quality or interest Inside, the walls
have been whitened light – a throwback to the fashion in the 1930s – let in by the
insertion of clear glass, and new furnishings have been introduced, although some
statues and a war memorial remain from the past. The altar and the font are of
concrete and are each raised on a red platform: the font has three sections, one a
stoup, one for infant baptism and one for immersion.

Reference: Pevsner, 5, p. 251.

St Mary, Plaistow

Status: in use.

Location: St Mary's Road, north side, near junction with Pelly Road.

Nearest station: Plaistow.

Constructed: 1981.

Architect: not known.

This was a replacement for a substantial church by Blomfield, which was closed in 1977. It is a featureless hall with sloping roofs, white walls, and little of interest within. The visual impact on the locality is very limited.

Reference: Pevsner, 5, p. 251.

St Matthias, Canning Town

Status: in use.
Location: Kimberley Road.
Nearest station: Canning Town.
Constructed: 1991.
Architect: APEC.

This is yet another replacement by APEC for an earlier and much larger church. The new church centre has a small and undistinguished worship area joined to rooms for community use and for housing the vulnerable. It is, like others of its type, of light brick and lacking any sort of originality or presence. The walls are unpainted and there is little by way of internal visual stimulation.

Reference: Pevsner, 5, p. 259.

St Michael & All Angels, Little Ilford.

Status: in use.
Location: Romford Road, corner Toronto Avenue.
Nearest station: Manor Park.
Constructed: 1990.
Architect: APEC.

This church forms part of the Froud centre, named after a local priest, and is kept open during the day because of the adjoining community facilities. It is a far more adventurous and successful building than many of those in the borough and is beautifully maintained. The exterior is of brick and immediately proclaims its presence by an external metal bell frame, and a large statue of St Michael and the serpent by Robert Crutchley. The main area has the altar along one of the longer walls, all the fittings being of matching wood. There is a separate chapel, modern windows of the Resurrection and of the Madonna and Child, and, somewhat incongruously, two windows of 1906 from the former church, together with war memorials. This is one of the more successful new buildings in the area and is now the parish church, with the ancient church of St Mary as its daughter.

Reference: Pevsner, 5, pp. 286-7.

St Paul, Stratford

Status: in use.

Location: Waddington Road, corner Maryland Road.

Nearest station: Maryland.

Constructed: 1952-3.

Architect: Humphreys & Hurst

This replaced a bombed Victorian church and was built in an area where there was widespread post-war reconstruction: it was one of the first new churches in East London. The main body of the building is dark brick on concrete panels with low-pitched roofs, and there are a substantial number of rectangular windows along the sides. The most striking feature of the church is the rectangular tower over the west entrance with a bellcote above, now without bells.

References: Pevsner, 5, pp. 224-5; SPWC, p. 18.

St Philip & St James, Plaistow

Status: in use.

Location: Whitwell Road, corner Foster Road.

Nearest station: Plaistow.

Constructed: 1954-5.

Architect: J. Harold Gibbons.

Harold Gibbons was a distinguished architect whose best work can be seen in the inter-war periods, such as St Francis of Assisi, Gladstone Park. He continued to build in a similar style after 1945, and this church therefore resembles one from an earlier era. Its predecessor, which was bombed, was used by the Order of the Divine Compassion, a community influenced by Franciscanism and Socialism, which has now become defunct: the parish is now named after it. Gibbons built in a very traditional form, and had a site large enough to enable him to do so. The nave and chancel are covered by one long roof, without the irritating changes of perspective caused in other places. There are transepts at the east end on either side, and an Italianate tower which stands to the north-west, near the entrance, and provides a readily identifiable message to the passer-by. There are fine details, such as an external stone carved calvary in a circle, which stands out against the light brick. Internally, there are many arches of different designs, and the white-painted walls and clear glass windows are more successful than in many places. The tradition has remained Anglo-Catholic and there are a variety of statues and the like: the high altar is under a high baldachino.

Reference: Pevsner, 5, p. 252.

Other Churches

St Alban, Upton Park

A substantial parish church was built in Wakefield Street from 1903, but was
not completed until 1934. It was restored in 1949 after being bombed, but was
demolished about 1975. A new building called St Alban's Christian Centre was
opened in 1980, but is no longer used regularly for Sunday worship. It used parts
of the former church hall.

St Edmund, Forest Gate

This is another APEC conversion: a church in Katherine Road dating from the
early twentieth century was demolished and replaced by flats. The former vicarage
was adapted for multiple uses with a church area in 1988 and in 1993-4 additions
were made to make it look more like a religious building, including a figure of
Christ from the old building.

226

St James, Stratford

This is a small outpost of the Evangelical St John, Stratford, in Alfred Road, Maryland. It is a low temporary looking building with no glamour.

St Mark, Forest Gate

Yet another APEC conversion to replace a demolished Victorian church, in 1987. This is a church and community centre, with the church behind: it incorporates a First World War memorial window from the former church. The church is conventionally white-walled and incorporates an immersion font.

Redbridge

St Francis of Assisi, Barkingside

Status: in use.

Location: Fencepiece Road, east side, south of Trelawney Road.

Nearest station: Hainault.

Constructed: 1957.

Architect: J.J. Crowe.

This is an astonishing church for its date. One of the last buildings designed by Crowe, it has a vaguely Spanish mission feel about it which jars somewhat with the local architecture and is redolent of buildings from the interwar period. It is brick-built with a tower at the west end which spreads on both sides over the entrance, and low aisles on the north and south sides of the nave. The church has a strongly Anglo-Catholic tradition which sets it aside from most of those around, and it supports Forward in Faith. It replaced a hall built between the Wars.

Reference: Pevsner, 5, p. 324.

St Paul, Hainault

Status: in use.

Location: Arrowsmith Road, between The Lowe and Agister Road.

Nearest station: Hainault.

Constructed: 1951.

Architect: not known.

The Hainault estate was an early post-war development and so this church was constructed very early in the period of local growth and fits in well with the area. It was the first church/hall in the Diocese of Chelmsford and thus established a precedent which was soon followed elsewhere. The church is a simple barn-shape, but with an arcaded porch over which there is small tower which stands out to the passer-by and has a clock beneath the copper flèche. The interior is bare and functional, but includes some items from bombed East End churches: the cross and candlesticks came from All Saints, Stepney and the organ from Bow. The church has always been ultra-Evangelical and was the subject of much attention during the ministry of the Revd Trevor Dearing (1970-5) when it was frequently packed. It has since returned to a less flamboyant existence.

Other Churches

St Clement, Great Ilford

After the demolition of the large Gothic church in Park Avenue in about 1977, the congregation moved in 1979 to the former church hall, a large Arts and Crafts-influenced building of 1907, which was adapted for services, but is no longer so used.

Richmond

St Augustine of Canterbury, Whitton

Status: in use.

Location: Hospital Bridge Road, on the roundabout with Great Chertsey Road.

Nearest station: Whitton.

Constructed: 1958.

Architect: Edward Maufe.

In 1958 a new church was constructed to replace a chapel in the premises of Bishop Perrin School which had been used since 1935. Sir Edward Maufe provided a building which bore some similarities to his masterpiece, St Thomas, Hanwell, which was contemporary with the former chapel. St Augustine is a substantial, extremely traditional, building on the very outskirts of the London area, with a massive tower and few internal concessions to the time it was erected. Maufe's skill shows in the use of space and in the well-proportioned arches which divide the nave from the aisles. The sanctuary is also conservative in execution and is well lit by the three-light east window behind.

St Mary, Barnes

Status: in use.

Location: Church Road, north side, east of junction with Kitson Road.

Nearest station: Barnes Bridge.

Reconstructed: 1980.

Architect: Edward Cullinan.

This ancient church, which has stood on the same site since the Domesday Book, was almost completely gutted by fire in 1978, leaving only the outer walls and the brick-built sixteenth-century tower. It was decided not to rebuild as before, but to replace the nave and chancel while using the south wall and some other remaining parts of the old building. A new wing projecting to the north was added which houses the altar: thus there is a curious amalgam of styles, which is not readily apparent from the south side. The entire building required a modern roof. The new wing has a plain modern slightly raised sanctuary beneath a pitched roof with curious internal projections.

References: Pevsner, 2, p. 468; Leonard, pp. 324-6.

St Peter & St Paul, Teddington

Status: in use.

Location: Church Road, corner High Street.

Nearest station: Teddington.

Constructed: 1980.

Architect: Biscoe & Stanton.

This church was erected to replace a relatively minor work by Street (1863-73): the old building had fostered a strong Anglo-Catholic tradition which has been maintained in the new. The font and some other furnishings including the memorials were moved into the new church. Biscoe & Stanton produced an uncompromisingly modern, perhaps now somewhat dated, outline with an extraordinary roof which from the outside resembles a giant water slide. Internally, it leads down to the sanctuary, which is thus made a focus and there is natural light from above: the chairs are arranged on either side with a central aisle way, rather than in auditorium-style as in many other places. There is a small stylised belfry and a number of modern stained glass windows. A number of traditional and modern statues and icons of the saints of the dedication are found.

St Richard, Ham

Status: in use.
Location: Ashburnham Road, opposite Broughton Avenue junction.
Nearest station: Richmond.
Constructed: 1966.
Architect: Ralph Covell.

This church and the adjoining primary school were constructed to serve the Riverside Estate, which was built 1961-8: it replaced an earlier temporary hut. The church was designed on a coherent pattern based on the six-pointed Star of David, with copper-coloured roofs and a tall but slight flèche above. The central area of the building, which is thus hexagonal, is used for worship and can be used for other activities and in the points of the star are various ancillary rooms, including a lady chapel, and the entrance. The stained glass was also designed as a whole, by Henry Haig, and depicts the life of the patron saint.

Southwark

All Hallows, Southwark

Status: disused and closed, awaiting development.
Location: Pepper Street, corner Copperfield Street.
Nearest station: Southwark.
Constructed: 1957.
Architect: T.F. Ford.

The noble Victorian church by George Gilbert Scott junior (1879-80) was gutted in the War: instead of rebuilding or demolishing, the Diocese adopted a halfway course of adapting one chapel into a new church, obviously meagre in comparison with what had gone before, designed by Ford, in the old garden. A new small bell-tower was added. The new church has, predictably, been made redundant and there are controversial plans to redevelop the whole site.

References: Pevsner, 2, p. 575; Clarke, pp. 263-4.

All Saints & St Stephen, Walworth

Status: now sold to, and used as the European headquarters of, the Church of the Lord (Aladura).

Location: Surrey Square, south side, east of the park.

Nearest station: Elephant & Castle.

Constructed: 1959.

Architect: N.F. Cachemaille-Day.

Cachemaille-Day produced here one of his later churches, which replaced a bombed building by Parris & Field of 1864-5. It was completed in 1959, closed as early as 1975 and by 1977 was being considered for demolition, but instead was sold to a Nigerian group, one of many in the area. The building, of yellow brick over concrete, is not as memorable as many by this architect: it resembles a warehouse from the front, in which there is a substantial window over the entrance. There are slit windows in the side, and at the east end an apse with curious small apertures near the ground. The reredos was by Christopher Webb. Some of the architect's furnishings were removed to the nearby St Peter, Walworth, when this building was closed to Anglican worship.

References: Pevsner, 2, p. 575; Clarke, p. 254.

Christ Church, Southwark

Status: in use.

Location: Blackfriars Road, west side, near junction with Colombo Street.

Nearest station: Southwark.

Constructed: 1959.

Architect: R. Paxton Watson and B. Costain.

Pevsner describes this as a 'feeble little replacement' for the church of 1671, remodelled in 1890, which was damaged in the War. That is somewhat unfair, although it is indeed a small building and is now dwarfed by the offices around. The parish population has largely disappeared and much of the ancillary accommodation is now let out. The church itself is of pale brick, the nave and chancel being barrel-vaulted. There is a clock tower of reasonable proportions and well-executed external detail around the windows and doors. Internally it was traditionally designed. The church has many stained glass windows, unusually for its date. The original set, by K.G. Bunton, are conventional in form and show local life over the years and local activities. In 1984–5 John Lawson designed a further set, which set out the changing parish in an unusual and interesting sequence.

Reference: Pevsner, 2, p. 575.

Holy Trinity, Rotherhithe

Status: in use.

Location: Rotherhithe Street, corner Bryan Road.

Nearest station: Surrey Quays.

Constructed: 1960.

Architect: T.F. Ford.

The former church was destroyed in bombing in 1940 and the present building was constructed in the same large garden. The area has changed very considerably since 1960, and is now far more prosperous than for many years. The church is typical of many Southwark replacements, namely constructed by Ford with an internal mural by Hans Feibusch. It is small, low and traditional in plan, constructed of pale brick with a pitched copper-covered roof. There are narrow aisles divided from the nave by simple columns, and an alcove sanctuary with the mural above the altar. There is a separate lady chapel at the west end. As with all Ford's churches the detailing is good and the building is exceptionally well-maintained.

References: Pevsner, 2, p. 598; Clarke, p. 261.

St Andrew, Waterloo
Status: demolished.
Location: Short Street, corner Ufford Street.
Nearest station: Waterloo.
Constructed: 1960.
Architect: D.E. Nye & Partners.
In the back streets near Waterloo Station, the Diocese of Southwark saw
fit to have built a traditionally designed church, as late as 1960. It had a
tower and a conservative internal plan, and was constructed of Wealden
bricks over a concrete frame structure with copper pitched roofs. As early
as 2003 it was declared redundant and soon thereafter demolished. In 2006
a new, much taller, building was erected which has many other uses but
incorporates a small worship area.

St Antony with St Silas, Nunhead

Status: in use.

Location: Ivydale Road, corner Merttins Road.

Nearest station: Nunhead.

Constructed: 2002–3.

Architects: Oliver West and John Scott.

This is a brand-new church which replaced St Antony (originally St Antholin), Nunhead Lane, which had been reconstructed by Laurence King in 1957 after being bombed, and was sold, and St Silas, Ivydale Road, which was demolished. It has a striking external appearance, assisted by its site, with a large tower with louvred windows at the top and plain glass lower down. Internally, it is surprisingly small but the small black wooden altar stands out as the focal point against the white walls. Most of the furnishings are contemporary, such as the fittings in the Blessed Sacrament chapel, but there are windows and statues from the previous churches. Most significantly, although somewhat incongruous, is the Wren reredos from the former City church of St Antholin, Watling Street, which was restored by Martin Travers just before the War, re-restored by Laurence King, and is now against one wall.

St Barnabas, Dulwich

Status: in use.

Location: Calton Avenue, east side, half way along.

Nearest station: North Dulwich.

Constructed: 1995.

Architect: L. Malcic of HOK.

The church of 1892-5 by W.H. Wood, of red brick with a substantial tower, was substantially destroyed by fire in 1992 and the remaining parts were then demolished, save for a small portion of the south aisle wall which was incorporated into the entrance area of the new building. The replacement is octagonal, with the altar placed centrally, which remains an unusual plan: the organ and choir stalls are in the east end. The centre of the church is a barrel vault with a glass spire above leading to a tapering octagon. The spire floods light into the area beneath. There is also modern stained glass by Caroline Swash. This is a much more original building than many.

Reference: Leonard, pp. 329-31.

St Clement, Dulwich

Status: in use.

Location: Friern Road, west side, between Underhill Road and Goodrich Road.

Nearest station: East Dulwich.

Constructed: 1957.

Architects: L.K. Hett and J.C.H. Odam.

St Clement is a typical church of its era, built on traditional lines in a pleasant suburban setting. The Liturgical Movement need never have happened. It is rectangular, with a broad but somewhat stubby tower at the west end, constructed of red brick and with a pitched roof to the nave and chancel but with flat-roofed aisles on either side, which give an odd outline externally. Internally it is pleasant and well kept, the conservative nature of the planning being demonstrated by the provision of a gallery at the west end and a separate chapel at the east end. There are a number of statues and some glass of indifferent quality, together with a rather better external wall figure of St Clement. Above the altar is an early glass and concrete cross.

St Crispin, Bermondsey

Status: used as a nursery school.

Location: Southwark Park Road, west side, south of junction with Jamaica Road.

Nearest station: Bermondsey.

Constructed: 1958-9.

Architect: T.F. Ford.

This church replaced a bombed Victorian church (1879-80 by Coe & Robinson). Its history is regrettably typical. It was not consecrated until 1959, by which time depopulation and changes in ethnic mix had already begun to make it surplus to requirements. It was made redundant as early as 1999 and is now a nursery. It is a standard production by Ford, and was provided with a mural by Hans Feibusch. The building is still in its original state externally, with a tall seven-light window with curved top looking out at the street and another at the side, and a tower with copper roof and interesting detail. Internally, the central area was square with a large arched sanctuary and a lady chapel with glass by M.C. Farrar Bell. It is a more interesting church than many which have survived in use.

References: Pevsner, 2, p. 599; Clarke, p. 202.

St Faith, North Dulwich

Status: in use.

Location: Red Post Hill, corner Sunray Avenue.

Nearest station: North Dulwich.

Constructed: 1958.

Architects: D.E. Nye & Partners.

This church showed that the Gothic tradition lived on far longer than sometimes imagined. It is not unfair to refer to it, as Pevsner does, as "debased", but it is effective, especially internally. The church is built opposite a hall which was formerly used for services. It is of red brick over concrete with a pitched roof and no tower. The nave has on each side three Gothic-style windows although the aisles on either side have much smaller rectangular apertures and there are no openings in the east or west end walls. The west wall has a fine external rood by Ivor Livi. The interior is stunning, with white walls and substantial concrete arches above, but with contrasting ceiling colours where appropriate. The surprising feature is the lady chapel, which is behind the high altar and which has a very good series of windows of saints by Lawrence Lee, contemporary with the construction.

St George, Camberwell

Status: in use.
Location: Coleman Road, opposite Dowlass Street.
Nearest station: Elephant & Castle.
Constructed: 1982.
Architects: Millard Wright & Wynn.

The former church of St George, erected in 1840, was declared redundant and allowed to fall into ruin before eventually being demolished. It was replaced by the Trinity College Centre which contains within it the new St George. The church area is quite small, but there are folding screens to the hall. The building from the outside looks unpretentious and there are some awkward roof lines, but it has a small bell-tower which is well detailed. Inside, the detailing is equally good although the walls have been left as unpainted brick. There are new stained glass windows by Henry Haig (1985) and behind the altar is hung a fine Travers crucifix which previously stood in front of the Wren reredos now in St Antony & St Silas, Nunhead. It also has a figure of St George by Laurence King in Travers style which was made for the reconstructed St Antholin, Nunhead, in 1957.

St John, Peckham

Status: in use.

Location: Meeting House Lane, corner Springall Street.

Nearest station: Queen's Road (Peckham).

Constructed: 1965.

Architect: David Bush.

This church was built on the site of the bombed church of St Jude (1875-6 by Blomfield). It is one of the earliest churches built in a contemporary rather than traditional style, and now looks rather as though some maintenance is needed. The red brick building itself seen from the outside would be conventional but for the roof. About one half of the pitched roof on the back rises up and joins a four part tower like structure, which proclaims the church's presence to the neighbourhood. Internally the main area is dark, which contrasts with the chapel of St Jude, which is lit by stained glass. Despite the modern appearance, the altar was not centrally placed but rather is on a small platform in the traditional way. The glass is by Susan Johnson and there is a fibreglass statue of Our Lady holding the Child above her, by Ron Hinton.

St Katharine with St Bartholomew, Rotherhithe
Status: in use.
Location: Eugenia Road, far end.
Nearest station: Surrey Quays.
Constructed: 1965.
Architects: Covell Matthews & Partners.
This church replaced an earlier building dedicated to St Katharine of 1884
by W.O. Milne. The nearby church of St Bartholomew was demolished in
1993. The church serves the Silwood Estate, but is hidden from the main
road and lacks any presence. The plan was traditional for the date, with
a long nave and chancel and a separate chapel to the south. Although a
nave altar has now been installed, an altar remains at the east end with a
powerful Christus Rex behind it. The brick building has an apse at the east
end and a smaller apse in the south chapel, together with a concrete loop
above the roof holding a bell. The most striking feature is that the nave
walls are in zig-zag formation, with windows containing abstract stained
glass by Carter Shapland. The internal walls are also plain brick. There are a
number of statues, reflecting a traditional Anglo-Catholic ethos.

References: Pevsner, 2, p. 599; Clarke, p. 261.

St Luke, North Peckham

Status: in use.
Location: Chandler Way corner Pentridge Street.
Nearest station: Peckham Rye.
Constructed: 1953.
Architects: A.C. Martin & R.B. Craze.
The recently refurbished North Peckham area has as its parish church this large neo-Byzantine church, one of the few in that style built after the War. It was designed by Martin but completed by Craze. It is in red brick, and has a large but relatively low central tower above the crossing, very high transepts on either side, and an apse behind the altar. There is a lady chapel to the south of the chancel. The interior is dominated by the traditionally styled reredos in the apse.

References: Pevsner, 2, p. 615; Clarke, p. 210.

St Mary, Newington

Status: in use.

Location: Kennington Park Road, east side, opposite Othello Close.

Nearest station: Kennington.

Constructed: 1958.

Architect: A. Llewellyn-Smith.

Here the church was bombed but the tower, on the main road, was left and now almost hides the new church, constructed in 1957-8. Although the building is quite low, it is well-designed and impressive from the outside, with a portico in front. The building is of brick with shallow pitched roofs: it is rectangular, but, ingeniously, the worship area is cruciform and each corner has ancillary accommodation. There is an apsed sanctuary and a traditional high altar with communion rails.

References: Pevsner, 2, p. 576; Clarke, pp. 250-1.

St Mary Magdalene, Peckham.

Status: in use.

Location: Dundas Road, corner St Mary's Road.

Nearest station: Queen's Road (Peckham).

Constructed: 2010-11.

Architects: IID Architects.

This is another place where a Victorian church was bombed, but the subsequent history has been illuminating. A new building was erected in 1962 designed by Potter & Hare: it was one of the first in London to follow the lead of St Paul, Bow Common in being designed in accordance with the provisions of the Liturgical Movement, albeit in this case within an Evangelical context. The church had a striking presence in an island in the road and was cruciform in shape, with four steeply gabled roofs of copper and very large windows. However, the promise of the new building was not fulfilled and it looked increasingly decrepit: the main problem was constant leaking from the roof, coupled with the fact that the large area of glass gave the building a greenhouse effect in the summer. In 2010 it was demolished, and on 7 May 2011 a new church and community centre was consecrated, this time of more conventional outline, with an auditorium like worship area with immersion font, lacking the originality of its predecessor but hopefully proving watertight.

St Matthew, Camberwell

Status: in use.

Location: Lilford Road, corner Coldharbour Lane.

Nearest station: Loughborough Junction.

Constructed: 1959.

Architect: Ralph Covell.

This is yet another replacement for a church bombed in the War, and yet another not constructed until 14 years after the cessation of hostilities. The reliable and safe architect Ralph Covell produced a traditional brick-built design with shallow pitched roof, nave and chancel and an adjoining hall divided by folding doors: the nave can also be divided from the chancel by further folding doors. There is an east window by John Hayward.

St Matthew, Newington

Status: in use.

Location: Meadow Row, corner St Matthew's Row.

Nearest station: Elephant & Castle.

Constructed: 1994.

Architect: Hans Haenlein

The church of 1867 by H. Jarvis, remodelled in 1926-7 by Martin Travers, and its hall, were demolished in the early 1990s in order to construct a replacement. This is a new low-build complex with a small worship area at the back and one stained glass window from the old church incorporated. There are a variety of other rooms adjacent. A small bell-tower by the gate is the only external indication that this is a religious building.

St Michael & All Angels and All Souls with Emmanuel, Camberwell

Status: in use.

Location: Wyndham Road, corner Comber Grove.

Nearest station: Oval.

Constructed: 1974.

Architects: Thomas F. Ford & Partners.

This church was built as part of a large complex which includes the Archbishop Michael Ramsey School. It is a small somewhat nondescript building from the outside, with walls in no particularly apparent pattern, but is surmounted by a spire filled with coloured glass. Internally, it is basically rectangular with a bright abstract window behind the altar and some abstract paintings.

St Paul, Newington

Status: in use.

Location: Lorrimore Square, in centre.

Nearest station: Kennington.

Constructed: 1959-60.

Architect: Woodroffe Buchanan & Coulter.

This is a listed building, still relatively rare for a church of its age. It replaced a bombed church by H. Jarvis. It is ambitiously planned, with the church above and ancillary accommodation below, thus elevating the building so that it is visible from the streets around. The exterior is somewhat challenging to the eye, with projections from the copper-coloured roof, and honeycomb patterned windows looking out onto the square. The interior is however considerably more conservative, with a long nave, transepts, an altar at the east end and a lady chapel behind it. There is a wealth of contemporary furnishings, including a statue of the Risen Christ by Freda Skinner and glass by Goddard & Gibbs. The interest of this building is greatly enhanced by the fittings of the same age.

References: Pevsner, 2, p. 577; Clarke, p. 254.

St Philip & St Mark, Camberwell

Status: in use.

Location: Avondale Square, far end.

Nearest station: South Bermondsey.

Constructed: 1963.

Architect: N.F. Cachemaille-Day.

This very late design by Cachemaille-Day, in the year of his retirement, replaced a bombed church of 1875. The quality shows in the careful and ingenious plan: the church itself is an octagon within a square building, so that the ancillary rooms such as a vestry can be accommodated within the corners. The church hall survived the blitz and has not been replaced. The surrounding estate is owned by the Corporation of London and the surroundings are noticeably neater than many places around. There is a pitched copper roof with small spire above. The interior is white and kept immaculate: there is a large painting of the Resurrection above the altar and angels on the ceiling, both by John Hayward and a window by Christopher Webb. The church retains an Anglo-Catholic ethos.

References: Pevsner, 2, p. 616; Clarke, pp. 211-12.

Other Churches

St Antony, Nunhead

This church by Laurence King (1957) was the reconstruction after bombing of a church by Ewan Christian. It was brick and barn-like, with a low range in front of the west wall. It was sold on the construction of the new church of St Antony with St Silas.

St John, East Dulwich

This church in East Dulwich Road was bombed but not destroyed in the War. J.B.S. Comper was appointed as architect very soon afterwards and as early as 1951 reconstructed the church, using what remained but raising the nave walls by 9 feet so as to insert a clerestory and change the roof profile. There are a number of furnishings reminiscent of the architect's more famous father and glass by Bucknall.

St Mary Magdalene, Peckham

The now demolished church by Potter & Hare (1962) is dealt with under the main entry.

Sutton

St Oswald, Cheam

Status: in use.

Location: Brocks Drive, corner Molesey Drive.

Nearest station: West Sutton.

Constructed: 1953.

Architect: Thomas F. Ford.

In 1936 a hall/church was built by T.P. Carr for this area, which was developed on the site of the Brock's Fireworks factory. The present church was added in 1953 but the hall remains. The building is typical of its age, being unobtrusive, traditional, and easy to maintain. It is brick-built with a pitched roof and shallow arches within: the sanctuary is in an alcove and there are many large clear windows.

St Paul, Roundshaw

Status: in use.
Location: Mollison Drive, opposite Lindbergh Road
Nearest station: Wallington.
Constructed: 2003.
Architect: K.C. White.

This area was developed on the site of the old Croydon Aerodrome. The first church here (by Pickford & Rose, 1980-1) was a simple building rather akin to a small warehouse, which had a tower on which was hung a cross made from an old aircraft propeller. The "propeller church" as it was then known had a remarkably short life, being demolished as part of general development and replaced by the present church, which is a joint venture with Baptists, Methodists and the URC. It retains the propeller cross, but as it is on the wall and there is now no tower it is far less visible. The building has an unecclesiastical appearance externally, with pitched roofs of unequal size, in order to include ancillary rooms: the worship area is simple and rectangular, with an alcove for the sanctuary and two Victorian stained glass windows adding some interest.

Tower Hamlets

All Hallows, Bromley-by-Bow

Status: in use.

Location: Devons Road, north side, corner Blackthorn Street.

Nearest station: Devons Road.

Reconstructed: 1955.

Architects: Caroe & Partners.

In 1873 Ewan Christian constructed on this site a substantial Victorian church with a sanctuary apse and a spirelet. The building was bombed out in 1940. In 1955 it was reopened as, in effect, a new building, although the architects were able to use part of the remaining structure, and in particular they kept the shape of the apse, although it was refenestrated. Unusually, a very much more substantial tower was added on the north east corner, which is far more imposing than the previous small spire. New wooden furnishings of high quality were provided. The work carried out by Caroe & Partners was done to a high standard and with originality: instead of a stock and heavy Victorian building the parishioners had a much lighter church with white walls and far more windows. The apse has five lancets with powerful contemporary glass by William Morris & Co. In place of the former massive piers the architects used slender columns, adding to the feel of spaciousness. The south aisle was not replaced but a north aisle and chapel was included. In 1999 a substantial refurbishment and reordering

took place under the direction of Keith Harrison Architects: a glass screen was introduced so that the church area was reduced to about one third of that provided in 1955 and the remainder used as a hall. The north aisle was divided off. The existing furnishings were used in the worship area but rearranged. The division of 1999 has been carried out much more sensitively here than in many cases.

References: Pevsner, 5, pp. 603-4; Clarke, pp. 166-7.

The Royal Foundation of St Katharine, Ratcliffe

Status: in use.

Location: Butcher Row.

Nearest station: Limehouse.

Constructed: 1950–2.

Architect: R.E. Enthoven.

The Royal Foundation of St Katharine is an extraordinary survival.
A religious community was established near the Tower in 1147 and
refounded in the late thirteenth century. Although it survived the
Reformation because it was a Royal Peculiar, its buildings were
demolished in 1825 for St Katharine's Docks but the Foundation was
re-established in Regent's Park. In 1914 it returned to the East End, and
after the Second World War it was decided to build on the site of the
former St James, Ratcliffe. The Master was then the Revd St John Groser,
a distinguished Anglo-Catholic priest of strong Socialist convictions who
was, like Father Conrad Noel at Thaxted, devoted to morris dancing. A
new chapel was erected in stock brick and was designed to be ready for
the Festival of Britain. The chapel was remarkable for its furnishings: it
accommodated some of the monuments and other artefacts which had
moved with the Foundation across London and back again, but it featured
a freestanding altar with a star shaped wrought iron corona above, the
work of Keith Murray, who was subsequently to become famous for his
work at St Paul, Bow Common. The drawings for the furnishings were
done by his partner to be, Robert Maguire. This altar was very advanced
for the Church of England at that time, although such altars were by then

increasingly being found in other countries in Roman Catholic churches. Father Groser's son Michael carved the very large wooden crucifix, which now hangs high on the wall. The chapel was reordered in 2003-4 by Christopher Smallwood Architects: the windows were enlarged so that they are now very substantial and have arched heads, and a new circular window was inserted in place of a concrete statue of St Katharine. New richly coloured stained glass windows by Alan Younger were erected. A new wooden reredos was erected in light wood and using Gothic forms: it holds within it a marble relief of the Adoration of the magi of uncertain provenance. The itinerant furnishings remain and some are of very high quality, albeit somewhat incongruous in the setting.

Reference: Pevsner, 5, pp. 519-22.

St Luke, Millwall

Status: in use, but with plans to replace it.
Location: Havannah Street, corner Alpha Grove.
Nearest station: South Quay.
Constructed: 1960.
Architect: not known.

The former church of St Luke, in what was one of the most deprived areas of London, was demolished in 1960 and replaced by a temporary hall/church, which is a small flat-roofed building. The parish hopes, now that the entire area has been transformed, to build a new permanent church to replace this building, which is increasingly difficult to maintain. It does however have a friendly interior, with some bright glass and some crude but powerful stations. There is an outside calvary from the old church.

St Mark, Old Ford

Status: used as a nursery.
Location: St Mark's Gate, corner Cadogan Terrace.
Nearest station: Hackney Wick.
Constructed: 1973–6.
Architect: not known.

This church centre and hall replaced a substantial building by Blomfield and was built as recently as 1973–6 for the Revd H.E. Roberts. It is of dark brick with slit windows, unobtrusive in appearance, and despite its recent date is now used as a nursery.

St Matthew, Bethnal Green

Status: in use.

Location: St Matthew's Row, east side.

Nearest station: Shoreditch.

Constructed: 1958–61.

Architect: Anthony Lewis.

This church externally is much as it was originally built by George Dance in 1743–6 for the weavers who then lived in Bethnal Green. In 1859–61 it was remodelled after a fire, and then in 1940 it was gutted, leaving it roofless. A temporary church was built within the walls, but instead of constructing a smaller replacement, as was done in so many other places around, it was decided to rebuild using the original drawings but to remodel entirely the interior. Thus what appears from the outside to be an eighteenth-century building is fitted with many furnishings of the mid-twentieth century, many of which reflect the Anglo-Catholic tradition of the church and others of which have been taken from closed churches in the area. The white painted walls allow the fittings to stand out. The architect, Anthony Lewis, designed some himself, such as the font and the tester above what was a very early free-standingaltar, with panelling by Robert Dawson. Behind the altar is a gallery reached by a staircase to the south which has very substantial reliefs of St Michael and the Devil by Kim James, and a timber Apostles' screen in the gallery shields an upper

lady chapel with semi-circular wall paintings by Barry Robinson. Laurence Lee designed the stained glass in the chapel of St Philip, one window of which has symbols of the lost churches of the locale and another of which is made up of fragments from the former church of St Philip.

References: Pevsner, 5, pp. 554–5; Clarke, p. 161.

St Nicholas & All Hallows, Poplar

Status: in use.

Location: Aberfeldy Street, corner Dee Street.

Nearest station: All Saints.

Constructed: 1953-5.

Architects: Seely & Paget.

This church was constructed in 1953-5 to replace the bombed churches of
St Nicholas and of All Hallows. It was a modest brick-built replacement,
with hall and clergy accommodation attached, and was closed in 1968
and used for almost 30 years as a store, but in 1997 was reopened and
has remained in use since that time. It is an interesting contrast with the
nearby St Paul, Bow Common, in that here the church is traditional in
plan and modest in its display to the passer-by. In 2002 it was reordered

by Keith Harrison Architects and a very plain sanctuary was set out,
reusing an earlier wooden altar which had been removed in 1968. There
is a small tower over the porch with a minute thin spire and some tall,
clear windows on the south side which allow a great deal of light to
penetrate. There is a stone Crucifixion outside and a statue of St Nicholas,
now inside but originally external, both by Michael Groser. The most
extraordinary feature is the painted ceiling by Brian Thomas. During the
1948 Lambeth Conference Seely & Paget, who were restoring the Palace,

used this to conceal repairs and it was then brought to Poplar. The ceiling shows angels and is a striking contrast to the rest of the furnishings. Three icons by Michael Coles were installed after the 2002 restoration.

References: Pevsner, 5, pp. 642–3; Clarke, pp. 167–8; SPWC, pp. 86–7.

St Paul, Bow Common

Status: in use.

Location: Burdett Road, corner St Paul's Way.

Nearest station: Limehouse.

Constructed: 1958-60.

Architects: Maguire & Murray.

There is no doubt that this is the best-known post-war church in London. Gerald Adler in his recent book on the practice of Maguire & Murray says it is: 'the most famous and significant parish church to be built in Britain in the latter half of the twentieth century. It crystallised architectural and theological thinking about the form the church should assume in the post-war era'. On the other hand, it is notoriously recorded that the scholarly antiquarian Revd B.F.L. Clarke recorded in his notebooks 'looks like a rather seedy stable-yard'. The church was undoubtedly ground-breaking, in that it turned into brick many of the principles of the Liturgical Movement, which had already been reflected in churches constructed on the continent, but, and this is often overlooked, did so within the context of the Anglo-Catholic practice of the idiosyncratic and anarchist parish priest, the Revd R. Gresham Kirkby, who was much involved with the design. He gave the commission for mosaics to Murray, who in turn introduced him to Maguire, who had no experience at all of designing or building churches. The partnership between Maguire and Murray had not been established at this stage and was not formed until construction had started: Maguire was still a very young man. The design was inside out: in other words it was centred on the altar and the church was built around that, rather than the other way about. Further, the main walls were unbroken by windows, all the light coming from above, and broken as little as possible by doors, although two chapels were provided, both arranged so

that celebration should take place facing east in the then conventional way. The high altar is centrally placed and not surrounded by any rail, but has a ciborium above it, and a corona. The church was deliberately arranged internally without barriers, clergy stalls, or the like. Above the altar is a brick cuboid with a lantern in turn topped by four equal roofs. One of the most prominent features, and one which formed part of the design from the very beginning, is that the roofs of the aisles overhang and have within them triangular gabled windows, over which the concrete roof is bent. The entrance to the church is by an octagonal porch and then past the font. The porch has bold lettering by Ralph Beyer, who had also worked at the Royal Foundation of St Katharine, proclaiming: 'This is the Gate of Heaven'. A substantial sum was given by the War damage Commission for mosaics, which were to replace stained glass lost in the destruction of the earlier church. These were to have been carried out by Murray, but in fact were carried out in 1963-8 by Charles Lutyens, great nephew of the architect, and represent angels at prayer. One of the aspects of the building which proved very controversial was the use of industrial materials, such as rough concrete, for the surfaces: however that has become accepted since, and this church has weathered well. It remains largely as built.

References: Pevsner, 5, pp. 606-7; Clarke, pp. 159-60; Leonard, pp. 315-7; G. Adler, *Robert Maguire & Keith Murray,* London, 2012, pp. 16-29; K. Leech, *Father Gresham Kirby 1916-2006*, London, 2009.

St Paul with St Stephen, Old Ford

Status: in use.

Location: St Stephen's Road, east side, north of Roman Road.

Nearest station: Bow Road.

Reconstructed: 2003.

Architects: Matthew Lloyd Architects.

The very large church by Newman & Billing, 1873–8, was radically reconstructed in 2003: the former very substantial nave has been diminished in size, not least by the insertion of a mezzanine supported on four stilts. The nave has also been cut short.

Reference: Pevsner, 5, p. 606.

Other Churches

St George-in-the-East, Cannon Street Road

Hawksmoor's great church of 1714-29, notorious as the scene of ritual riots in the nineteenth century, was gutted in the war. The exterior has been restored and in 1960-4 Ansell & Bailey erected within those walls a small modern church, a courtyard, flats and a hall.

St Peter's Barge, Limehouse

In 2003 a floating church was established in Hertsmere Road, West India Quay, as an Evangelical outpost for those working in Canary Wharf. It is now the only such church in London and is a reconstructed Dutch barge.

Waltham Forest

All Saints, Leyton

Status: in use.

Location: Capworth Street, north side, near junction with Welbourne Road.

Nearest station: Leyton Midland Road.

Constructed: 1973.

Architect: Laurence King & Partners.

This church replaced a Victorian building. At one time it was used as a nursery, but was then refurbished for use as a church again. It has very steeply pitched glazed roofs on either side of triangular walls at each end, which give it a slightly unusual appearance.

Reference: Pevsner, 5, p. 726.

Holy Trinity & St Augustine of Hippo, Harrow Green

Status: in use.

Location: Holloway Road.

Nearest station: Leyton.

Constructed: 1973.

Architect: Gerald Goalen.

The construction of this church was part of the regeneration of the whole area, which involved the demolition of many homes as well as the two existing churches of Holy Trinity and St Augustine, which were closed in 1973 and 1974 respectively. The sale of the two sites paid for the new building and the long serving vicar, the Revd Dennis Pearce, was closely involved in the planning, with the architect. It was designed to fit in with the Cathall Estate which was built around it: the result was a stark, windowless exterior from which the only projections are a bellcote on the roof and a small west porch surmounted by concrete depictions of the Trinity. The appearance led one newspaper to dub it 'the cube church'. However, inside natural light comes from strategically placed windows in the roof and the design is original yet understated. The church was built to reflect the changes in liturgical practice which had taken place, and the importance of the visibility of the solid marble altar was accentuated by the provision of a raked floor for the congregation and a platform for

the sanctuary. Some furnishings, such as the stations, were new: others, including a number of statues, came from the former churches. There is a small south chapel with Victorian windows depicting SS. Augustine, Alban, Bernard and Dunstan, which came from the closed Anglo-Catholic citadel of St Augustine, Haggerston. Instead of being a 'hall church', this was part of a complex which included a hall, parish office and vicarage.

Reference: Pevsner, 5, p. 734.

St Anne, Chingford

Status: in use.

Location: Larkshall Road, east side, south of junction with Hatch Lane.

Nearest station: Highams Park.

Constructed: 1953.

Architect: Foster & Tooley

This is a new church constructed relatively shortly after building recommenced following the War. It is of red brick, with a substantial and perhaps comparatively oversized tower at the west end. The tradition is one of Evangelicalism. The design is redolent of the characteristically tentative and conservative approach to the provision of new churches in the 1950s.

Reference: Pevsner, 5, p. 713.

St Francis, Hawkwood

Status: in use.
Location: Hawkwood Crescent, corner Epping Glade.
Nearest station: Chingford.
Constructed: 1951.
Architect: Unknown.
This was an even earlier building than the nearby St Anne. It has no architectural pretensions at all, being domestic in appearance and on the edge of open country. It is a hall church with some extensions, in brick. It is a daughter of Chingford Parish Church.

Reference: Pevsner, 5, p. 713.

Other Churches

St Andrew, Higham Hill
In 1988 APEC extended a hall in St Andrew's Road to form an ecumenical church centre for Anglicans and Baptists: a worship centre was constructed off the hall.

St Stephen, Walthamstow
In 1994 APEC built this small replacement dual purpose building in Copeland Road. Its tradition is Evangelical.

Uniting Church, Chingford Hatch
A long low brick building was constructed in Connington Crescent, Highams Park, for Anglicans and Methodists. It is now overgrown and disused.

Wandsworth

All Saints, Battersea

Status: in use.

Location: Prince of Wales Drive, south side, near junction with Queenstown Road.

Nearest station: Battersea Park.

Constructed: 1976–8.

Architect: David Gill.

This church replaced a building by F.W. Hunt of 1882–3, which was destroyed by fire in 1969. The site was used for housing and the new church constructed where the hall had stood. The brick-built building is somewhat jumbled in appearance, with offices facing the road, but has a striking clerestory tower above which lights the sanctuary. Within, the space has been effectively used so that various parts can be combined. Some stained glass from the former church has been incorporated.

Reference: Pevsner, 2, p. 667.

Christ Church & St Stephen, Battersea.

Status: in use.

Location: Battersea Park Road, corner Cabul Road.

Nearest station: Clapham Junction.

Constructed: 1959.

Architect: Thomas F. Ford.

This building is one of the more successful post-war churches built in a traditional style, not least because of the accumulation of interesting furnishings it now contains. Ford designed a brick church with a barrel roof and flat-roofed extensions on either side, to replace a bombed Victorian church. There is a campanile to the north and a concrete relief on the west wall. The interior was planned traditionally, with aisles on both sides, and as is often the case in the Southwark Diocese, a mural by Hans Feibusch behind the altar. On the closure of St Stephen, Battersea, the altar and rails by Martin Travers were moved here, together with the crucifix from the high altar reredos, which is now in the north chapel, near a statue of St Stephen which is in fact by Francis Stephens but in the Travers style. There is also a sacrament house by Stephens. The church has an atmosphere of holiness which it is rare to find in a building of its date.

Reference: Pevsner, 2, p. 667.

St Alban, Streatham Park

Status: in use.

Location: Pretoria Road, south side, between Moyser Road and Thrale Road.

Nearest station: Streatham.

Constructed: 1988.

Architect: Kemplin Iliffe & Partners.

This church replaced a Victorian church by E. H. Martineau which was demolished in 1986. It is brick-built with a number of ancillary rooms on the same site. The exterior has a curious array of windows and a downward projecting roof. The interior has brick walls and an auditorium effect as often found in modern Conservative Evangelical churches.

St Faith, Wandsworth

Status: in use.
Location: Ebner Street, corner Fullerton Road
Nearest station: Wandsworth Town.
Constructed: 1988.
Architect: Hans Haenlein.

This small yellow brick church, now a daughter of St Anne, Wandsworth, was constructed as part of a much larger project involving the demolition of the Victorian church and school on the site. The new church can be joined to the school hall if required. It is a simple low building with exposed joists from the roof and an altar positioned forward to be visible to all.

St George with St Andrew, Battersea

Status: in use.

Location: Patmore Street, corner St George's Close.

Nearest station: Queenstown Road (Battersea).

Constructed: 1996.

Architect: Levitt Bernstein Associates.

The Victorian churches dedicated to both St George and St Andrew were damaged by bombing and demolished. They were replaced in 1955-6 by a church by Covell Matthews & Partners which had a prominent copper-coloured spire over the porch to a substantial building with five bays in the nave and a sanctuary which was raised and lit from above: there was glass by W. Carter Shapland. The building was too ambitious for the area, and in 1996 it was replaced by a newer smaller building, at low level, but retaining the tower from the 1956 church. The latest church is a simple rectangular construction with wooden joists above, which reuses some of the glass.

St Mary, Putney

Status: in use.

Location: Putney High Street, east side, near Putney Bridge.

Nearest station: Putney.

Reconstructed: 1982.

Architect: Ronald Sims.

This mediaeval church was the subject of an arson attack in 1973. The tower, some of the nave arcading, and the Bishop West Chapel remain: the remainder of the church was the subject of an extremely extensive rebuilding. In the course of that, a new altar was installed, with corona above, both designed by the architect, and the sanctuary was moved to the north aisle, with the congregation in a semi-circular arrangement around it. New abstract stained glass by Alan Younger was installed. The former south aisle was adapted for use as ancillary rooms and the former church hall was incorporated into the new building. This is one of the most substantial rebuildings in the post-war period.

Reference: Pevsner, 2, pp. 680-1.

St Stephen, Wandsworth

Status: in use.

Location: Manfred Road, corner St Stephen's Gardens.

Nearest station: East Putney.

Constructed: 1981.

Architect: Melhuish & Anderson.

The Victorian church on this site, usually known as St Stephen, East Putney, was demolished in 1979 and the new building was erected on part of the site. It is a single-storey brick building holding 130 as opposed to the 450 who could be accommodated previously. It has a hall divided by a partition from the worship area and an apse behind the altar. There is a dormer window to light the church.

Other Churches

St Peter, Battersea

The church by William White in Plough Road was destroyed by fire in 1970, leaving only the tower, which was itself demolished in 1994. The congregation moved into the former school, to which was added in 1974 a small church/hall.

Westminster

Emmanuel, Paddington

Status: in use.

Location: Harrow Road, opposite Ashmore Road.

Nearest station: Westbourne Park.

Constructed: 1995

Architect: Peter Makower.

A rather dull Victorian church was replaced here, ingeniously, by housing into which was incorporated a much smaller church, reached through an arch in the centre of the new building. The simple interior with top light and a small apse incorporates a number of windows and other furnishings from the former church.

Guards' Chapel, Wellington Barracks

Status: in use.

Location: Birdcage Walk, south side.

Nearest station: St James's Park.

Constructed: 1961.

Architect: Bruce George.

For obvious reasons, there is very little modern religious architecture in central Westminster. A flying bomb largely destroyed the previous chapel in 1944 but the architect was able to incorporate into the new building an apse by Street (1877-9) and a cloister by Goodhart-Rendel (1954-5), which formed part of an earlier rebuilding scheme which was later abandoned. The new building has expanses of shimmering white walls. The basic design is of a rectangle, but there is a small bellcote above. There are slit windows in the north side of the nave, and lighting from above, and in the south side of the nave are six chapels, one for each Guards' Regiment. The interior incorporates decoration from the earlier chapel but there are also modern additions, such as screens by Geoffrey Clarke, and engraved glass.

Reference: Pevsner, 6, pp. 691-2.

St Luke, West Kilburn

Status: in use.

Location: Fernhead Road, corner Kilburn Lane.

Nearest station: Queen's Park.

Constructed: 1959.

Architect: Michael Farey.

This church demonstrates that new ideas were coming forward even at this relatively early date. This church is uncompromisingly modern in its construction: a low building with a central raised lantern and clerestory windows, with a tall copper spire above which makes it a landmark. It has been reordered since opening and the liturgical east is now west. The interior is relatively Spartan, but the church has a very fine collection of stained glass in the clerestory, unusual for its date, by Francis Spear, a former assistant to Martin Travers.

St Paul, Portman Square

Status: used as a conference centre.
Location: Robert Adam Street, corner Manchester Street.
Nearest station: Bond Street.
Constructed: 1970.
Architect: Green Lloyd & Adams.
This parish is merged with All Souls, Langham Place, and the church, built
only in 1970, is not now used for worship except by a Spanish Evangelical
group. It presents an almost unbroken façade of pale brick and concrete
to the outside world, and the interior is now a cleared large hall but with
some stained glass and mosaics, and a startling tester above the pulpit.
There are some memorials and the like from the former church.

Reference: Pevsner, 3, p. 603.

St Peter, Paddington

Status: in use.

Location: Elgin Avenue, corner Chippenham Road.

Nearest station: Westbourne Park.

Constructed: 1974.

Architect: Biscoe & Stanton.

This is a redevelopment of the site of a Victorian church to provide a small hall/church, flats, and ancillary accommodation. The church is dwarfed by the housing, despite a tower. It is lit from above by one window and is furnished simply, but with a fine statue of the patron saint. It is part of the parish of St Mary Magdalene and a greater contrast between this and that huge confident Victorian edifice is difficult to imagine.

Reference: Pevsner, 3, pp. 677-8.

St Saviour, Paddington

Status: in use.

Location: Warwick Avenue, corner Clifton Gardens

Nearest station: Warwick Avenue.

Constructed: 1976.

Architect: Biscoe & Stanton.

This is a local landmark, as was its Victorian predecessor, although much smaller than the building it replaced on Warwick Avenue: flats were also built on the site. Biscoe & Stanton made the new church much taller than in many of their designs, and then added a high glass fibre spire, rising from among brick piers. There are many high windows, and a considerable quantity of stained glass by John Hayward: the interior is restless and perhaps less than comforting. There is a gallery at the west end.

Reference: Pevsner, 3, p. 678.

Other Churches

St Anne, Soho

The former church, off Wardour Street, has been redeveloped around the tower after bombing. The new work includes a small chapel with plain wooden furniture, rededicated in 1991.

St Peter, Eaton Square

This fashionable church in Belgravia, constructed to a classical design by Henry Hakewill in 1824-7, was burned out by an arsonist in 1987 and rebuilt by the Braithwaite Partnership to a remodelled pattern, cool and white.

ARCHITECTS AND THEIR LONDON CHURCHES 1946-2012

Churches are listed with their district and London Borough

ALEXANDER, C.
1972-5: St George & All Saints, Tufnell Park, Islington

ALLEN, J.
1987-8: St Cuthbert, West Hampstead, Camden

ANSELL & BAILEY
1953-5: St Mary, Shortlands, Bromley
1960-4: St George-in-the-East, Cannon Street Road, Tower Hamlets

APEC
1983: St Bartholomew, East Ham, Newham
1987: St Mark, Forest Gate, Newham
1988: St Andrew, Higham Hill, Waltham Forest
1988: St Edmund, Forest Gate, Newham
1989: St Mark, Beckton, Newham
1990: St Michael & All Angels, Little Ilford, Newham
1991: St Matthias, Canning Town, Newham
1994: St Stephen, Walthamstow, Waltham Forest

ATKINSON, J.R.
1958: St Katharine, East Acton, Hammersmith

BARRINGTON-BAKER, J., & PARTNERS
1953-4: St Giles, Enfield, Enfield

BISCOE, G.
1953: St Augustine, Wembley Park, Brent (with W. W. Todd)
1955-8: St Etheldreda, Fulham, Hammersmith

BISCOE (M.) & STANTON
1971-7: St Paul, Tottenham, Haringey
1974: St Peter, Paddington, Westminster
1975: St Augustine, Grahame Park, Barnet
1975-6: St Clement, Fulham, Hammersmith
1976: St Saviour, Paddington, Westminster
1977: St Luke, Finsbury, Islington
1978: Holy Trinity, Swiss Cottage, Camden
1980: St Peter & St Paul, Teddington, Richmond

BLEE, M.
1967-70: All Saints, Isleworth, Hounslow
1990: St Paul, Brentford, Hounslow

BRAITHWAITE PARTNERSHIP
1988-91: St Peter, Eaton Square, Westminster

BROWN, J., & KERR, R.
1989: Christ Church, East Greenwich, Greenwich

BUSH, D.
1965: St John, Peckham, Southwark
1965-72: St Matthew, Croydon, Croydon
1976: St Mark & St Margaret, Plumstead, Greenwich

CACHEMAILLE-DAY, N.F.
1952: All Saints, Hanworth, Hounslow
1957-8: St James, Clapham Park, Lambeth
1958: St Mary, West Twyford, Ealing
1958-60: St Paul, West Hackney, Hackney
1959: All Saints & St Stephen, Walworth, Southwark
1959-61: St Michael & All Angels, London Fields, Hackney
1960: St Peter, Lee, Greenwich
1963: St Philip & St Mark, Camberwell, Southwark
1964: St Edmund the King, Northwood Hills, Hillingdon

CADBURY BROWN, H.T., & PARTNERS
2000: St John with St Andrew, Chelsea, Kensington

CAROE & PARTNERS
1951-3: Ascension, Pollards Hill, Merton
1955: All Hallows, Bromley-by-Bow, Tower Hamlets
1958: St Edward King & Martyr, New Addington, Croydon

CHANNING, L.
1964: St Richard of Chichester, Hanworth, Hounslow

COMPER, J.B.S.
1951: St John, East Dulwich, Southwark
1954-6: St Helen, North Kensington, Kensington
1958: St Matthew, Wimbledon, Merton
1958: St John the Evangelist, Coulsdon, Croydon

COOK, G.
1971: St Michael, Hatcham

COTTRELL & VERMEULEN
1991-7: St Martin, Plaistow, Newham

**COVELL, R.G.C. (or COVELL & MATTHEWS or COVELL
MATTHEWS & PARTNERS)**
1949: Holy Cross, Motspur Park, Merton
1953: St Francis, Eltham, Greenwich
1955-6: St Alban, Mottingham, Greenwich
1955-6: St George with St Andrew, Battersea, Wandsworth
1956: St Agnes, Kennington Park, Lambeth
1957: St Michael, Hatcham, Lewisham
1959: St Matthew, Camberwell, Southwark
1961: St Mary, Charlton, Greenwich
1965: St Katharine with St Bartholomew, Rotherhithe, Southwark
1966: St Richard, Ham, Richmond
1967-8: St Laurence, Catford, Lewisham

CRAZE, R.B. (MILNER & CRAZE)
1953: St Luke, North Peckham, Southwark (with A.C. Martin)

1954: All Saints, Queensbury, Brent
1958: St Cuthbert, North Wembley, Brent
1960: St Anne, Poole Park, Islington
1960: St Mark, Surbiton, Kingston-on-Thames
1967: St Thomas, Kensal Town, Kensington
1969: St Peter & St Paul, Enfield Lock, Enfield

CROSS, W.E.
1961: Holy Trinity, Hounslow, Hounslow

CROWE, J.J.
1952-3: St George, Harold Hill, Havering
1953: St Paul, Harold Hill, Havering
1955-6: St Nicholas, Elm Park, Havering
1957: St Francis of Assisi, Barkingside, Redbridge

CULLINAN, E.
1980: St Mary, Barnes, Richmond

CURTIS GREEN, SON & LLOYD (later GREEN, LLOYD & ADAMS)
1956: All Saints, Spring Park, Croydon
1970: St Paul, Portman Square, Westminster

DENMAN, J.L.
1952: St George, Shirley, Croydon

DRURY, B.
1987: Christ Church, Gipsy Hill, Lambeth

DYKES-BOWER, S.E.
1953-62: St Vedast, Foster Lane, City

ENTHOVEN, R.E.
1950-2 Royal Foundation of St Katharine, Ratcliffe, Tower Hamlets

FAREY, M.
1954-6: St Andrew, Roxbourne, Harrow
1956: Good Shepherd, West Hounslow, Hounslow

1959: St Luke, West Kilburn, Westminster
1964: Christ the Redeemer, Southall, Ealing

FORD, T.F. (after 1971 THOMAS F. FORD & PARTNERS)
1953: St Oswald, Cheam, Sutton
1954: St Mary, Welling, Bexley
1956-7: All Saints, Shooters Hill, Greenwich
1956-7: Good Shepherd, Lee, Lewisham
1956-7: St James, Morden, Merton
1957: St Peter, Bexleyheath, Bexley
1957: All Hallows, Southwark, Southwark
1958: St Michael & All Angels, Harrow Weald, Harrow
1958-9: St Crispin, Bermondsey, Southwark
1959: Christ Church & St Stephen, Battersea, Wandsworth
1960: Holy Trinity, Rotherhithe, Southwark
1974: St Michael & All Angels & All Souls with Emmanuel, Camberwell, Southwark
2004-5: St George, Perry Hill, Lewisham
2006: All Saints, West Dulwich, Lambeth

FORREST, J.
1968: St George, Heathrow, Hillingdon

FOSTER & TOOLEY
1953: St Anne, Chingford, Waltham Forest
1954: St Erkenwald, Barking, Barking
1957: All Saints, Squirrels Heath, Havering

FOWLER, C.W.
1954: St Mary of Nazareth, West Wickham, Bromley

FREEBOURNE, B.
1970: St Mary, Lower Edmonton, Enfield

GEORGE, B.
1961: Guards' Chapel, Wellington Barracks, Westminster

GIBBONS, J.H.
1954-5: St Philip & St James, Plaistow, Newham

1957: Ascension, Preston, Brent
1957: St Peter & St Paul, Bromley, Bromley

GILL, D.
1976-8: All Saints, Battersea, Wandsworth

GOALEN, G.
1973: Holy Trinity & St Augustine of Hippo, Harrow Green, Waltham Forest

GOLDSMID, I.
1986: St Stephen, West Ealing, Ealing

GOODHART-RENDEL, H.S.
1954: St Mary, Isleworth, Hounslow

HAENLEIN, H.
1988: St Faith, Wandsworth, Wandsworth
1994: St Mary, Newington, Southwark

HAINES, NORMAN, DESIGN PARTNERSHIP
1970: Holy Angels, Cranford, Hounslow

HALL, R.
1982: St James, Hatcham, Lewisham

HARRISON, K.
1988: Emmanuel, Upper Holloway, Islington

HEAL, V.
1957-8: St Augustine, Bromley Common, Bromley

HETT, L.K., AND ODAM, J.C.H.
1957: St Clement, Dulwich, Southwark

HINTON, BROWN, MADDON & LANGSTONE
1976-8: St Paul, Thamesmead, Greenwich

HOBDAY, W.H., & MAYNARD, F.J.
1955-6: St Michael & All Angels, Beckenham, Bromley

1955-6: St Michael, Lower Sydenham, Lewisham

HORNSBY, T.
1995: St John the Evangelist, Brownswood Park, Hackney

HURST, R.F. (or HUMPHREYS & HURST)
1952-3: St Paul, Stratford, Newham
1968-9: St Mark, Wimbledon, Merton (with D.E. Nye & Partners)
1973: St Matthias, Colindale, Barnet

HUTCHISON, LOCKE & MONTE
1967: Emmanuel, West Dulwich, Lambeth

HYSLOP, G.
1957-8: All Saints, Orpington, Bromley

IID ARCHITECTS
2010-11: St Mary Magdalene, Peckham, Southwark

JENKINS, P.
1988-93: St Paul, Harringay, Haringey

KEMPLIN ILIFFE & PARTNERS
1988: St Alban, Streatham Park, Wandsworth

KENYON, A.W.
1957: St Antony, Sanderstead, Croydon

KING, L. (or LAURENCE KING & PARTNERS)
1957: St Antony, Nunhead, Southwark
1959: St Mary, South Ruislip, Hillingdon
1963: St Mary & St Nicholas, Perivale, Ealing
1968: St John, North Woolwich, Newham
1973: All Saints, Leyton, Waltham Forest

KNAPP-FISHER, A.B.
1959: St Paul, Crofton, Bromley

LEVITT BERNSTEIN ASSOCIATES
1996: St George with St Andrew, Battersea, Wandsworth

LEWIS, A.
1958-61: St Matthew, Bethnal Green, Tower Hamlets
1961: St Edmund of Canterbury, Yeading, Hillingdon
1961: St Nicholas, Hayes, Hillingdon

LLEWELLYN-SMITH, A.
1958: St Mary, Newington, Southwark
1958: St Stephen, Canonbury, Islington

LLOYD, MATTHEW, ARCHITECTS
2003: St Paul, Old Ford

LOWE, GEORGE & PARTNERS
1959: St Barnabas, Purley, Croydon

LYON, RICHARD, & ASSOCIATES
1995-6: Ascension, Victoria Docks, Newham

MAGUIRE & MURRAY
1958-60: St Paul, Bow Common, Tower Hamlets
1967: St Joseph the Worker, Northolt, Ealing

MAKOWER, P.
1995: Emmanuel, Paddington, Westminster

MALCIC, L.
1995: St Barnabas, Dulwich, Southwark

MARSH, J.
2002: St Luke, Cranham Park, Havering

MARTIN, A.C.
1953: St Luke, North Peckham, Southwark (with R.B. Craze)

MARTIN-SMITH, D.F. (or BRADDOCK & MARTIN-SMITH or BRADDOCK, MARTIN-SMITH & LIPLEY)
1956: St Paul, Barking, Barking
1958: Little St Peter, Cricklewood, Barnet
1964: St Andrew, Sidcup, Bexley

MAUFE, E.
1957: St Alphege, Edmonton, Enfield
1958: St Augustine of Canterbury, Whitton, Richmond

MELHUISH, N., OR MELHUISH ANDERSON
1981: St Stephen, Wandsworth, Wandsworth
1984: St Philip the Apostle, Sydenham, Lewisham
1989: Immanuel & St Andrew, Streatham, Lambeth

MILLARD WRIGHT & WYNN
1982: St George, Camberwell, Southwark

MONK, A.J.
1976-8: St Luke, Shepherd's Bush, Hammersmith
1985: All Saints, South Acton, Ealing

MORRIS, R.S.
1957: St Andrew, Alexandra Park, Haringey
1959: St Mary with St George, Hornsey, Haringey

NELLIST, I.
1970: St Hugh of Lincoln, Northolt, Ealing

NORMAN ASHLEY GREEN
1969: St Stephen, South Lambeth, Lambeth

NORTHOVER & NORTHOVER
1962: St Francis, Selsdon, Croydon

NYE, D.E., & PARTNERS
1953: St Mark, Bromley, Bromley
1954: St Swithun, Purley, Croydon
1957: St Edward, Mottingham, Bromley
1958: St Faith, North Dulwich, Southwark
1960: St Andrew, Waterloo, Southwark
1968-9: St Mark, Wimbledon, Merton (with Humphreys & Hurst)

PICKFORD & ROSE
1980: St Paul, Roundshaw, Sutton

POTTER & HARE
1962: St Mary Magdalene, Peckham, Southwark

PRATLEY, A.J.
1974: Emmanuel, Southall, Ealing

PURCELL MILLER & TRITTON
1998: St Ethelburga, Bishopsgate, City

RILEY & GLANFIELD
1961: Annunciation, South Kenton, Brent
1982: Christ Church, West Green, Haringey

ROUSE, A.
1990: St James, Alperton, Brent

SCOTT, R.G.
1957-9: St Mark, Biggin Hill, Bromley

SEELY & PAGET
1952: St Michael & St George, White City, Hammersmith
1953-5: St Nicholas & All Hallows, Poplar, Tower Hamlets
1960: St Andrew, Holborn, City
1960-1: St Mary, West Kensington, Hammersmith

SIMS, R.
1982: St Mary, Putney, Wandsworth

SOPER, J.
1958: St Paul with St Saviour, Brixton, Lambeth

STARLING, E.F.
1962-4: St Barnabas, St Paul's Cray, Bexley

SUTTON-SMITH, F.
1957: St Martin, Morden, Morden

TAYLOR, M.
1991: Christ Church, Croydon, Croydon

THOMPSON & WHITEHEAD
1963: St Cedd, Becontree, Barking

TO, F.
1977: Risen Christ & All Souls, Clapton Park, Hackney

TODD, W. W.
1951: St George, Biggin Hill, Bromley
1953: St Augustine, Wembley Park, Brent (with G. Biscoe)

WATSON, R., PAXTON & COSTAIN, B.
1959: Christ Church, Southwark, Southwark

WATSON, RICHARD, & PARTNERS
1982: All Saints, Clapham Park, Lambeth
1990: Christ Church, Anerley, Bromley

WEST, O., AND SCOTT, J.
2003: St Antony & St Silas, Nunhead, Southwark

WHITE, K.C.
1962: Emmanuel, Morden, Morden
2003: St Paul, Roundshaw, Sutton

WOODROFFE BUCHANAN & COULTER
1959-60: St Paul, Newington, Southwark

WYLDE, RONALD, & ASSOCIATES
1957: St John & St Matthew, South Hornchurch, Havering
2000; St Luke, Canning Town, Newham

Index